American Authors and the Literary Marketplace since 1900

JAMES L. W. WEST III

upp

University of Pennsylvania Press / PHILADELPHIA

Library of Congress Cataloging-in-Publication Data

West, James L. W.
    American authors and the literary marketplace since
1900.

    (A. S. W. Rosenbach fellowship in bibliography)
    Bibliography: p.
    Includes index.
    1. Literature publishing—United States—History—
20th century.   2. Authors and publishers—United States—
History—20th century.   3. Authorship—History—20th
century.   4. American literature—20th century—
History and criticism.   I. Title.   II. Series.
Z479.W43   1988   070.5'0973   88-20620
ISBN 0-8122-8114-4

Printed in the United States of America

FOR
EMILY ARCHER WEST

Contents

Acknowledgments

I began this book in 1981–82 as a Fellow at the National Humanities Center. I wish to thank the administrators and staff members there who provided support—particularly Kent Mullikin and Wayne Pond, who organized a conference at the Center during the spring of 1982 on authorship in America. I am also grateful to the Fellows of my class for their suggestions and their company. I especially thank those who participated with me in a seminar on The Idea of a Profession—Gregory Vlastos, William Banks, Gilbert Sewall, Anthony LaVopa, and Edmund Pincoffs.

I am grateful to the University of Pennsylvania Library, to its former Director, Richard De Gennaro, and to its Assistant Director for Special Collections, Daniel H. Traister, for giving me the opportunity as Rosenbach Fellow during the spring of 1983 to refine early versions of some of these chapters for public presentation. I wish also to thank the American Philosophical Society for a travel grant, which made possible extended research trips to New York, Princeton, New Haven, Washington, D.C., and Charlottesville in 1983–84.

Much of the revision of this book was carried out during a year as Guggenheim Fellow and Fulbright Senior Research Scholar at Cambridge University, where I was also a Visiting Fellow at Clare Hall. I am most grateful to these institutions for their support. Finally I wish to thank the Institute for the Arts and Humanistic Studies at The Pennsylvania State University, and its director Stanley Weintraub, for assistance during the last stages of manuscript preparation.

Among friends I wish to thank James O. Hoge, Christopher Clausen, Arthur D. Casciato, Arthur B. Evans, and Lee Ann Draud for reading the manuscript at various stages and making useful suggestions. Sandra Stelts discovered the illustration for the dust jacket. LaVerne Maginnis and Robert Myers assisted with the proofing and the index. Jane and Bill Wilkins were most hospitable during several research trips to New York City, as was Richard Lingeman; Evie and Don Reymond were similarly hospitable in London. My thanks to them all.

J. L. W. W. III
University Park
November 1987

The fact is that authorship is guilty of a great mistake, a gross want of tact, in formulating & publishing its claim to be a "profession." Let other trades call it so—& let it take no notice. That's enough. It ought to have of the professions only a professional thoroughness. But *never* to have that, & to cry on the house-tops instead that it *is* the grocer & shoemaker is to bring on itself a ridicule of which it will simply die.

—Henry James to Edmund Gosse (10 May 1895)

Profession. In my passport I am down as "university professor." That was a convenience for 1926, when I first took it out. I thought of putting "writer," but people who are concerned with passports have complicated reactions to the word.

—Robert Graves (1929)

Introduction

This book is an examination of authorship and the literary marketplace in America since 1900. I have concentrated on the careers of novelists, poets, and short-story writers and have given relatively little attention to journalists, dramatists, and screenwriters, although I have examined the careers of several poets and fiction writers who worked as journalists, served stints in Hollywood, or wrote occasionally for the stage. Several well-known authors are treated—Theodore Dreiser, Robinson Jeffers, Edith Wharton, F. Scott Fitzgerald, E. E. Cummings, Flannery O'Connor, William Styron, and James Dickey, for example—but the commercial pressures felt by these authors were felt also by other writers whose names are less familiar today. I have therefore given attention to such authors as George Barr McCutcheon, John P. Marquand, Ida Tarbell, Stephen Vincent Benét, Ogden Nash, Edna Ferber, William Saroyan, Booth Tarkington, and Zona Gale. I have drawn on published sources and on the surviving papers of authors, publishers, editors, and literary agents. The resulting book is an attempt to describe the changing professional situation that faced the serious author in America after 1900 and, on occasion, to show how that situation affected the author's writings and career.

The informing principle of the book is my belief that if scholars or critics are fully to understand works of literary art, they must understand the commercial factors that influenced the composition and publication of these works. Ideally scholars and critics should know more about the literary marketplace of the author's time than the author would have known. The marketplace was only one of several factors that influenced the literary work, of course, and sometimes it was only a minor factor, but it was never absent from the author's thoughts if that author proposed to earn a living by writing. Commercial factors often influenced the published form of the work, and its success, more than the author realized.

Goethe said that true genius reveals itself best when it operates within limitations. He was speaking of the formal limitations of poetry—rhythm, rhyme, and stanzaic form—but he could as easily have been speaking of the commercial and legal limitations under which any artist works. The application of Goethe's principle to literary work should be self-evident, but perhaps some examples from other fields, such as architectural history, will help make the point. Most students of twentieth-century American culture see the great Art Deco skyscrapers erected in New York City between 1925 and 1931 as magnificent expressions of the wealth, success, arrogance, frivolity, and gaucherie of the American twenties. The Chrysler Building and the Empire State Building are the two best-known examples: viewed in purely aesthetic terms they are often seen as embodiments of the American will to achieve, to rise, to better oneself, to outdo one's competitors. The architects and designers who produced these structures and others of the period are said to have captured (perhaps even epitomized) the spirit of their times. In retrospect their buildings have become symbols of one of the most glamorous eras in American history.

One cannot fully understand the appropriateness of New York's Art Deco skyscrapers and the genius of their design, however, without knowing in some detail the municipal regulations and economic restrictions that existed when they were built. Because land values were soaring in Manhattan during the late 1920s, new office buildings had to be designed to provide maximum rental space. Immediate return on capital investment was crucial to the owners of these buildings. If it had been possible, these designers would probably have erected huge boxlike structures in order to take advantage of every possible square foot of aerial space. Later, of course, this is precisely what happened with the International Style, but in the late 1920s air-conditioning had not been perfected, and architects had to keep buildings narrow enough to provide adequate cross-ventilation.

New York municipal zoning ordinances were important. For example, these ordinances required that buildings be designed with setbacks, beginning at heights determined by the widths of the streets that the buildings were to face, so that daylight would not be blocked from the streets. Part of any building could be of unlimited height, but here, too, economics were a factor. If a building were extended to an extreme height, too much space on the lower floors would be taken up by elevator shafts. At a certain point, more height actually produced less rentable square footage. Exterior ornament had also to be applied with economics in mind. The most desirable and prestigious offices in a skyscraper are corner offices because they command views in two directions. Architects normally make these offices larger than those along the sides of the building; the combination of extra floor space and additional sunlight makes corner offices rent for considerably more per square foot—an economic factor on which skyscraper owners learned early to rely. Architects were therefore under orders, when designing skyscrapers, to keep wide or elaborate ornament off the corners of the buildings.

Zoning laws and economic factors thus combined to encourage the erection of a particular kind of structure: a tall, clean-cornered, ziggurat-crowned prism rising out of a broad base and usually topped by a tower or by two towers erected side by side. The wide, poorly ventilated base of the building was used primarily for heating and plumbing systems and for maintenance and storage. The central tower functioned as income-producing office space. We have come through hindsight to see these structures as soaring, clean-lined embodiments of the spirit of the twenties, but the architects who originally designed them had to take other, more mundane ideas into account as they worked. Legal, structural, and economic limitations were in many ways as important to them as were aesthetic considerations.[1]

The principle operates also in sculpture and painting. The example of the ceiling of the Sistine Chapel is a familiar one; Michelangelo had to design and execute his figures within the already existing beam-and-vault structure of the roof. Less well known is the history of his statue of David, which he carved from a block of marble that Bartolomeo di Pietro had spoiled in Carrara and from which the sculptor Agostino di Duccio had already begun to fashion his own David. Michelangelo's figure had to be designed and sculpted around the inherent limitations of the spoiled block of stone and the subtractions made from that block by di Duccio.[2]

The principle operates in less elevated forms of art. One of the most difficult transitions for early jazz musicians, for example, was between jam sessions and recording sessions. Riff-chorus compositions in jazz usually begin with a vamp and end with an outchorus or tag, but the number of ensembles or solos within either the twelve-bar blues or the thirty-two-bar pop forms can be altered. In jam sessions, the solos and ensembles often extend indefinitely, but for 45-RPM recordings they

1. Cervin Robinson and Rosemarie Haag Bletter, *Skyscraper Style: Art Deco, New York* (New York: Oxford University Press, 1975).

2. Ludwig Goldscheider, *The Sculptures of Michelangelo* (London: Allen and Unwin, 1940), pp. 9–10.

must be confined within approximately a three-minute limit. Even for 33⅓ RPM recordings they must be structured to fit a period of roughly ten minutes. This is done by retaining the riff-chorus structure but experimenting with, and "concentrating," the solos and ensembles.[3]

The parallel with literary work should be clear. Critics have the luxury of interpreting the writings of earlier generations solely as aesthetic entities, but the authors who produced these writings had to do so with both artistic and practical motives in mind. They had to create within the limitations and strictures imposed on them by the markets to which they sold their work. These limitations influenced virtually everything with which authors had to concern themselves—subject matter, tone, language, content, characterization, length, balance between narration and dialogue—all features that might affect the publishability or subsequent salability of an item.

Nearly all practicing teachers and critics in the field of American literature today are children of the New Criticism; in consequence, most of them were not encouraged during their apprenticeships to view works of fiction and poetry as items of literary merchandise. Most graduate students today are similarly uninformed about the mechanics of the publishing industry and the workings of the literary marketplace. This book is meant to supply working teachers and their graduate students with some basic information about the economics of authorship in America during this century. It is also meant to encourage them to go farther—to learn, on their own, more about the American literary marketplace and its effects on individual authors and their writings. This book should encourage teachers and students to be alive to, alert to, the manifold commercial influences that operate in literature; it should foster a habit of mind, a willingness to view literary works as both aesthetic entities and salable wares.

Parts of this book were delivered originally as the Rosenbach Lectures at the University of Pennsylvania during the spring of 1983. These sections, especially chapters 1–3, still retain much of their character as lectures: they are general and suggestive; they deal more with ideas than with data. The next four chapters are more narrowly topical and more closely based on archival research. The final chapter is again general: here I attempt to bring together some of the threads of discussion that have

---

3. Albert Murray, *Stomping the Blues* (New York: McGraw-Hill, 1976), pp. 177–78.

been developed in earlier chapters. None of these chapters, however, is magisterial in scope; I have not begun to cover in depth all aspects of the business of authorship in America since 1900. The time has not yet come for a full-scale history of literary authorship in this country during the twentieth century. The topic is vast, and the century has several years to run. More important, there is as yet relatively little post–1950 archival evidence available for study—a fact reflected in the coverage I am able to provide, especially on the editor and the agent. I hope some day to write that full-scale history for the entire century; in the meantime, I should like for this book to be viewed as a beginning effort in that direction.

William Charvat, whose work I admire, made distinctions among "private" authors, "public" authors, and "mass" authors. Like Charvat, I am chiefly interested in the "public" author, the serious literary artist who meant also to reach a large audience through the publishing apparatus of the time and who wanted to earn a living by writing. I have attempted to describe in this book some of the conditions under which such an author worked in America during this century. My author was not a Kafkaesque hunger artist or a Chekhovian dance pianist. Instead my author was a combination of the two authorial figures in John Fowles's *The French Lieutenant's Woman*. The first of Fowles's alter egos is the stern, inquisitive, blunt-mannered literary man who rides in the first-class compartment with Charles Smithson on his trip from Lyme to London. The second is the goateed and be-ringed dandy who stands across the street from the Rossetti house in London and puts into motion the alternate ending of the novel. My author, the one whose career I examine here, is a blending of these two characters—simultaneously an artist and an impresario, an aesthete and an entertainer, a thinker and a businessman.

Chapter 1

Authorship

> Mr Coleridge is of that description of persons, who fall
> within the notice of your benevolent Institution. He is a man
> of undoubted talents, though his works have been unpro-
> ductive, and, though he will in future be able to support
> himself by his own industry, he is at present quite un-
> provided for, being of no profession.
>
> —Letter to the Royal Literary Fund
> on behalf of S. T. Coleridge (13 May 1796)

Authorship in America during the twentieth century has been, strictly
speaking, neither a profession nor a trade. This situation has caused difficulty for authors who have attempted to support themselves by full-time
writing. Since the Industrial Revolution, the major strategy for organizing white-collar labor within a democracy has been professionalization;
the primary method of organizing blue-collar labor has been unionization. Most workers in the literary marketplace—publishers, literary
agents, and printers—have become highly organized during this century,
and authors have had to deal with them, directly and indirectly, in order
to transform unpublished fiction and poetry into salable merchandise.
Publishers and agents, though not true professionals, have been among
the most visible of the quasi-professionalized classes; printers, who are
true tradesmen, have historically been among the best organized and
most effectively unionized groups within the labor force. Authors, however, have been neither true professionals nor true tradesmen, and as
a consequence they have found it difficult to combine for business purposes or even for the creation of collective identity. They have been
neither professionals nor proletarians: they have instead occupied an
anomalous and uneasy economic position in American society, a circum-
stance that has affected their choice of audience, their selection of material, and their sense of mission. It is important at the beginning of this
study to examine the author's status within the economy, for much of
what follows can be understood only if one grasps the fact that authors
are economically classless.

Most American authors since 1900 have wished for something like professional status within the culture, but nearly always they have been disappointed. Theodore Dreiser, facing debt and nervous prostration in 1903 after the *Sister Carrie* debacle, regretted the impracticality of his gifts. "The uselessness of speculation!" he lamented. "Would that I had a vast fund of technical information."[1] Authors, Dreiser had learned, do not possess marketable qualifications or funds of useful data in the same way that professionals do. A professional has knowledge of a specialized body of information and applies it to the affairs of others. Divinity, pedagogy, law, and medicine are the original professions, but many other fields have become quasi-professionalized in America during this century. White-collar workers have been quick to recognize the benefits of a professionalized job structure, and they have patterned their apprenticeship systems and business associations after those of physicians and attorneys.

Professions in this country originally grew out of the middle classes and came to be a kind of substitute for British class structure. The professions began formally to organize in America during the late 1840s and grew in importance with the developing American bourgeoisie during the last half of the nineteenth century. The American Medical Association, for example, was chartered in 1847, the American Bar Association in 1878, and the Modern Language Association in 1883. The professions rose steadily in importance and public regard during the early decades of the twentieth century, and today they dominate the career thinking of many Americans.

True professions have several common characteristics. Candidates must be trained for entry: they serve educational apprenticeships and internships, they pass qualifying examinations, and they are issued licenses to practice. Certification procedures are important because the status of a profession depends largely on the ease of entry to and exit from it. Within each profession there are hierarchies, titles, and status levels—some of them obvious to outsiders, others apparent only to the initiated. Members of true professions are required to join associations and to follow written codes of ethics; they are also expected to command specialized terms and vocabularies beyond the understanding of lay audiences.

Partly as a result, the professional-client relationship is *fiduciary;* that is, the dealings involve trust and, quite often, confidentiality of commu-

---

1. *American Diaries, 1902–1926,* ed. Thomas P. Riggio et al. (Philadelphia: University of Pennsylvania Press, 1982), p. 104, entry for 11 February 1903.

nication. The professional always retains the upper hand. *Black's Law Dictionary,* in defining a fiduciary relationship, explains that "on the one side there is an over-mastering influence, or, on the other, weakness, dependence, or trust, justifiably reposed." Clients are considered subordinates and are almost never allowed to participate in their own cases. Fiduciary relationships are usually based on the fact that the profession is a monopoly with strong economic power. Crucial to the establishment of a profession, in fact, is its success in persuading a legislative body to grant it a legal monopoly. Ideally, from the professional's perspective, the practice of a profession without certification should be a criminal act. Professionals will thus be insulated from the pressures of a free-enterprise marketplace, and it will be relatively easy for them to minimize competition and fix fees.[2]

It should be obvious that authors in America during the twentieth century have not enjoyed professional status. Indeed, their status in this country has historically been uncertain. During the seventeenth and eighteenth centuries Americans took their ideas about writers from the British, who thought of literary authorship as a pastime for spare moments, one of the areas in which the gentleman or courtier was expected to be proficient. A strong taint was attached to publication, and several of the greatest British poets of the period published almost no verse during their lifetimes. Writers who did publish usually did so anonymously or pseudonymously, and with elaborate (though sometimes hollow) disclaimers. The notion of the author as leisured gentleman, of course, was partly myth. There were successful full-time authors in Elizabethan and Jacobean England: for every Sir Philip Sidney there was a William Shakespeare; for every Henry Howard, Earl of Surrey, there was a Ben Jonson. Shakespeare and Jonson, however, derived their principal incomes from aristocratic patrons or from performance of their work, not from the sale of their writing in printed form.[3]

This notion of the author as amateur, with its overtones of dabbling and dilettantism, was a great hindrance to such early American writers

2. The seminal study of the rise of professionalism is A. M. Carr-Saunders and P. A. Wilson, *The Professions* (Oxford: Clarendon Press, 1933). A useful collection of readings is *Professionalization,* ed. Howard M. Vollmer and Donald L. Mills (Englewood Cliffs, N.J.: Prentice-Hall, 1966). For information about the professions in America see Burton J. Bledstein, *The Culture of Professionalism* (New York: Norton, 1976).

3. See J. W. Saunders, *The Profession of English Letters* (London: Routledge and Kegan Paul, 1964), chaps. 3–4.

as Joel Barlow, Lemuel Hopkins, Robert Treat Paine, Jr., and Joseph Dennie. "Literary" composition was considered by most Americans to be an idle pursuit, something undertaken to amuse oneself and one's friends. There was strong disapproval of commercial publication and of the notion of earning money for literary work. Even during the first half of the nineteenth century, when the image of the author was changing in British society, Americans continued to cling to vestiges of the British model. This was illogical, of course, because the United States had no class of patrons to support its would-be authors. A few had supporters from the wealthy mercantile classes, but most earned their bread by labor other than writing. Typically they were clergymen, teachers, attorneys, or editors, and their principal energies and freshest hours were devoted to these occupations.

American writers of the eighteenth and early nineteenth centuries were also hampered by the fact that U.S. copyright laws were weak, and trade in the manufacture and sale of books by native authors was mostly unprofitable. The book-publishing industry was slow to establish itself in the United States. Most colonial publishers were little more than job printers who operated on financial shoestrings. They were unwilling to risk what little venture capital they had on the efforts of native Americans. Much of their publishing was religious or utilitarian in character, and if they did publish verse or prose narrative, they preferred to pirate from established British authors, whose work was more likely to sell. The native poet, novelist, or essayist either had to pay for his or her own work to be printed and bound or had to acquire a patron or locate subscribers who would provide a subvention. Distribution was a serious problem, and advertising was scanty. Because the domestic publishing trade could not support a class of full-time authors, the American writer had little status or dignity. An author was a "poor scribbling wretch" who hid behind pseudonyms or couched imaginative writing in elaborate narrative frames. The only advantage these authors had over their successors was that they could meet and deal with publishers on approximately equal terms.[4]

American authors chafed under such status, and by the 1830s Ralph

---

4. William Charvat, *Literary Publishing in America, 1790–1850* (Philadelphia: University of Pennsylvania Press, 1959), pp. 17–26 and 42–55; idem, *The Profession of Authorship in America, 1800–1870* (Columbus: Ohio State University Press, 1968), chaps. 2, 3, and 10. For a more recent and to some degree revisionist treatment, see Cathy N. Davidson, *Revolution and the Word: The Rise of the Novel in America* (New York: Oxford University Press, 1986), esp. chaps. 1 and 2.

Waldo Emerson was trying to establish a Coleridgean "clerisy" of letters in this country. Emerson and his fellow Transcendentalists attempted to found such a secular clerisy in New England, where they envisioned a literary and philosophical group existing within a strong mercantile society and supported by it. They almost succeeded in their efforts. Tocqueville, however, had already recognized that a popular democracy such as the United States would never support its authors as readily as a traditional aristocracy would. A free-enterprise system, he predicted, would shift to the public much of the burden of philanthropy in the arts, and the public would be an indifferent benefactor. Support would be concentrated on music, painting, and sculpture rather than on literature; and the greatest interest would be reserved for artists who were no longer alive.[5]

By 1835, when Tocqueville published the first two volumes of *Democracy in America,* conditions were beginning to improve slightly. The United States had had a domestic copyright law since 1790: the provisions of this law were not especially generous, but they did give the status of property to creative literature. A poem or a novel could be regarded under the law as an article of commerce that could be made to yield profit. During the 1820s and 1830s both James Fenimore Cooper and Washington Irving did well as full-time authors, and publishers like Mathew Carey and his traveling booksellers (among them Mason Locke Weems) attacked problems of promotion and distribution with some success. From 1854 on, Longfellow was able to support himself from the proceeds of his pen; after the Civil War, writers like Bret Harte, Mark Twain, and William Dean Howells flourished, partly because of the growth of the magazine market late in the century. International copyright legislation came in 1891, with the literary agent setting up in America shortly thereafter. By 1900, native trade publishers, grown prosperous from textbook sales and from their earlier transatlantic piracies, were more frequently willing to take chances on creative work, either to enhance their reputations or to gamble on possible best-sellers. All of these developments helped to improve the status of American authors but only because their publishers were now more successful and powerful.

Through it all, authors as a class remained unorganized, and the public

5. Lewis P. Simpson, *The Man of Letters in New England and the South: Essays on the History of the Literary Vocation in America* (Baton Rouge: Louisiana State University Press, 1973), pt. 1, "The New England Ideal"; Alexis de Tocqueville, *Democracy in America* (New York: Harper and Row, 1966), pp. 432–35, 438–43.

continued to regard authorship as less than serious work. The author occupied a vaguely defined position: there was no established training program to complete, no license to acquire in order to practice, no formal
hierarchy of ranks or titles to pursue, and few clearly identified goals toward which to strive. Writers in America did not provide a utilitarian service to society in the same way that doctors or lawyers did, and they
wielded no specialized technical vocabulary. They were required to follow no firm code of ethics; all that was necessary was that authors refrain
from plagiarizing other authors and avoid libel suits.

If authors were not professionals, then were they tradesmen? The des-
ignation would seem apt: trade workers perform skilled labor for which
they must be trained, and, like authors, they often work on a free-lance
basis for numerous employers. Unlike authors, however, true tradesmen
attempt to limit the labor supply. They exercise control over who enters
their ranks, either by choosing who will be apprenticed or by select-
ing who will be admitted to their labor unions. These unions provide fel-
lowship, a system of ranks and seniority, and insurance and retirement
schemes. Because tradesmen in unions have a monopoly on certain types
of labor, they influence not only wages and working conditions but also
rates of productivity and pricing. Literary authors no doubt would like
to think of themselves as tradesmen. Theodore Dreiser, recalling his
futile efforts to find work while trying to recover from neuresthenia,
wrote, "In that hour I wished a hundred times that I had learned some
trade which I could now turn to. It would have saved me so much pain."[6]

Authors, however, are not tradesmen. Economically they are more
closely akin to common laborers, who can control entry into their occupations (and thus control wage levels) only when they work in closed
shops and are fully unionized. Most authors, by contrast, work alone and
are averse to unionization. Professional associations and trade unions develop legally protected monopolies on certain services, and they cooper-
ate in fixing fees. But no author in a democracy can have a monopoly on
the written word. Authors cannot fix remuneration because they cannot
control supply. The most they can do, through their associations, is to
agitate for sets of standard contractual terms or insist on minimum basic
agreements.

British authors historically have found it easier to organize for collec-

6. *An Amateur Laborer*, ed. Richard W. Dowell et al., Pennsylvania Dreiser Edition
(Philadelphia: University of Pennsylvania Press, 1983), p. 129.

tive action than have American authors. Indeed, the Society of Authors in Great Britain is probably the most successful writers' association in the history of literary authorship. The Society was founded in 1884, and after an uncertain first few years it began to gather membership, money, and influence. From the beginning, important authors associated themselves with the group; among the first to affiliate were Matthew Arnold, T. H. Huxley, James Anthony Froude, Wilkie Collins, Charles Reade, W. S. Gilbert, John Ruskin, and W. M. Rossetti. The first president of the Society was the Poet Laureate, Alfred Tennyson.

Initially, a major function of the Society was to demystify publishing for its members—to rid them of the notion that it was a cult with secrets open only to those in the industry and to urge them to read and question their contracts before signing them. The Society caused publishers to eliminate some of their more unpopular practices (the "thirteen-for-twelve" discount to booksellers, for example) and helped persuade them to abandon the half-profits system, which was fair in theory but open to abuses in practice. Disputes between authors and publishers were routinely mediated by the Society, and its members were influential in bringing about passage of the Net Book Agreement in 1899.

Novelist Walter Besant, diplomatic and tireless, was the guiding spirit of the Society of Authors until his death in 1901; G. B. Shaw, energetic and witty, led the Society during the decade that followed. Both men campaigned against the notion that authorship was not real work. Shaw in particular helped educate the British public about the difficulty and precariousness of full-time writing, and he made some headway against the common conception of authors as dilettantes and hobbyists. Since the 1920s the Society has come increasingly to resemble a massive literary agency with some of the characteristics of a trade union. In fact, the Society had itself declared an independent trade union, for political purposes, in 1978. Its presence and activities help to explain why British authors have had a stronger sense of social identity and common cause during this century than have their American brethren.[7]

Organizations for American authors have existed since the late nineteenth century, but they have not been especially influential on authors as a class, or on the publishing industry. William Dean Howells recognized the problem and as early as 1904 began to advocate that organizations of

---

7. An excellent history of the Society is Victor Bonham-Carter's *Authors by Profession*, 2 vols. (Los Altos, Calif.: William Kaufmann, 1978, 1984).

both publishers and authors be established. In an article in *Harper's Weekly,* he made these suggestions:

> I hope I am not working treason to my own calling in suggesting to publishers the formation of a syndicate pledged among its members to the payment of such and such prices to authors, and vowed to an absolute constancy in one another's behalf, and to an unrelenting warfare upon all publishers outside of the syndicate who offer different terms. It might not work at first, but perhaps it would work at last. Then there would be nothing for the authors but to form a labor-union, with a schedule of prices for fiction, history, poetry, psychology, travel sketches, reviews, and so on, and all sorts of penalties, direct and indirect, for ratting authors.[8]

There were already loosely organized groups of authors in America when Howells wrote these words, but they did not develop into the trade unions he envisioned or even into associations as strong as the Society of Authors. The Association of American Authors, for example, was founded in 1892; it survived for ten years and was replaced by the Authors League of America. (That group today is an umbrella organization for the Authors Guild and the Dramatists Guild.) There was not much effort among authors to organize during the 1920s, but the politically conscious 1930s produced the Newspaper Guild, the Screen Writers Guild, the Writers Union, the Unemployed Writers Association, and the highly visible League of American Writers, which held national congresses in 1935, 1937, 1939, and 1941. None of these groups had the influence of the Society of Authors in Great Britain, however, nor did any one of them produce a leader comparable to Besant or Shaw.

One example from the late 1940s helps point up the difficulties that American authors have faced when they have attempted to organize. American novelist and screenwriter James M. Cain made a vigorous effort in 1946 and 1947 to found a group that he wanted to call the American Authors Authority. It was Cain's belief that writers' associations had been ineffective in the past because they had attempted to organize personnel rather than literary property. Cain's solution was to form a centralized authority that would employ a "tough mug" to represent members in contract negotiations and in court. Such an organization would also give writers a voice in congressional investigations. Most authors readily agreed with Cain but stumbled over his final requirement—that members sign over all of their copyrights to the AAA. Cain's reasoning was

---

8. "A Painful Subject," *Harper's Weekly* 48 (9 Jan. 1904): 48.

sound: "Legally," he wrote, "it will be necessary, in order to accomplish what I have in mind, for writers to assign their copyrights to the Authority, as trustee, so that it does not go into court amicus curiae, at the court's pleasure, but as the plaintiff or defendant, as the case may be, since it will be the legal owner of the copyright."[9] Cain published a detailed plan for his AAA in the July 1946 issue of the *Screen Writer,* but he drew heavy criticism in the national press for the leftist nature of his proposals. He traveled and spoke on behalf of the AAA, and he wrote numerous letters to prospective members, but in the end he failed to attract more than a handful. Robert Hughes founded a rival organization, the American Writers' Association; this sparked debate for a few months, but eventually both groups died out. Cain was irked and disillusioned: "I come to the conclusion that writers, who are behind an 8 ball a mile high, cannot be organized," he wrote to one of his correspondents. "Plumbers, yes. But not 100% idiots."[10]

Today American authors can join such large organizations as Poets & Writers, Inc., the Authors Guild, Inc., the American Society of Journalists and Authors, Writers Guild of America (for screenwriters), P.E.N., and the fledgling National Writers Union. They can also affiliate with regional groups such as the Washington Independent Writers and the San Francisco Media Alliance. These groups keep authors in contact with one another and provide financial and contractual advice, but they are not true trade unions. Writers' unions are difficult to form in any case because they face certain inherent problems. What, for example, do writers organize for? Whom do they organize against? What collective power do they wield? How can they strike? Who is allowed to join? How can one persuade the most successful and visible authors, who do not stand to benefit much from membership in writers' groups, to join them? Writers, like laborers, can organize most effectively when they work in shop situations. American newspaper reporters and Hollywood scriptwriters, for example, have organized successfully during this century. Authors can

9. Cain to Mrs. William Donahey, 11 November 1946, James M. Cain Papers, Manuscript Division, Library of Congress, Washington, D.C.

10. Cain to Cyril Clemens of the International Mark Twain Society, 18 August 1947, Cain Papers. There is other information on Cain's AAA in Box 1 of the collection. For information on the dispute over Cain's plans, see Harrison Smith's editorial "The Authority," *Saturday Review of Literature* 29 (28 Sept. 1946): 18; also see the published debate between Cain and James T. Farrell entitled "Do Writers Need an 'AAA'?" *Saturday Review of Literature* 29 (16 Nov. 1946): 9–10ff. For information about the rival American Writers' Association, see the *New York Times,* 8 May 1947, p. 14.

also function well together if they have shared interests and markets; one of the most active and homogeneous groups today is Mystery Writers of America, Inc. Most novelists and poets work alone, however, and defend their individuality and privacy with great energy. Attempts to organize them for collective bargaining have nearly always failed.

For these various reasons, the position of the creative author in America has remained uncertain, neither high nor low. Howells, in his 1893 essay "The Man of Letters as a Man of Business," had hoped that this was only a transitional state and that eventually the author would be better integrated into his society:

> He is really of the masses, but they do not know it, and what is worse, they do not know him; as yet the common people do not hear him gladly or hear him at all. He is apparently of the classes; they know him, and they listen to him; he often amuses them very much; but he is not quite at ease among them; whether they know it or not, he knows that he is not of their kind. Perhaps he will never be at home anywhere in the world as long as there are masses whom he ought to consort with, and classes whom he cannot consort with. The prospect is not brilliant for any artist now living, but perhaps the artist of the future will see in the flesh the accomplishment of that human equality of which the instinct has been divinely planted in the human soul.[11]

Howells probably knew that he was being overly optimistic. American authors who have followed him have had no firmly established economic or social position. In academic and belletristic circles some of them have been respected, honored, and even revered; but in society at large most of them have been virtually unknown. Many have been tempted to echo Nathaniel Hawthorne's familiar and melancholy complaint: "It is a good lesson—though it may often be a hard one—for a man who has dreamed of literary fame, and of making for himself a rank among the world's dignitaries by such means, to step aside out of the narrow circle in which his claims are recognized, and to find how utterly devoid of significance, beyond that circle, is all that he achieves, and all he aims at."[12]

Any examination of the finances and status of authorship in America must include consideration of the publishing industry, which produces and markets the literary artifact. It is important, therefore, to note that

11. The essay was collected by Howells in *Literature and Life* (New York: Harper and Bros., 1902); it first appeared in *Scribner's Magazine* 14 (Oct. 1893).

12. "The Custom-House," in *The Scarlet Letter*, Centenary Edition (Columbus: Ohio State University Press, 1962), pp. 26–27.

publishing is one of the American industries that has gone to greatest lengths during this century to professionalize itself, or at least to take on the outward signs of professionalization. Eighteenth-century American publishers, of course, did not think of themselves as professionals. Most of them had few intellectual pretensions and did not consider themselves cultural gatekeepers or arbiters. There was no sense of publishing as a profession and little cooperation to maintain price levels. Competition was often murderous, and printer-publishers frequently went bankrupt. Early publishers were really unorganized tradesmen who combined the functions of printing, publishing, and bookselling under one roof. That condition persisted in various arrangements throughout much of the nineteenth century, with important publishers like the Harpers, Appletons, and Scribners operating their own printing plants and maintaining large retail bookstores. The printing and merchandising functions gradually fell away from most American houses during the last few decades of the nineteenth century, however, and by 1900 much printing and binding was jobbed out, and most bookselling was handled by separate firms.

Partly as a result, the status of publishers began to rise considerably around the turn of the century. They had begun to think of themselves as quasi-professionals by then: they no longer considered themselves manufacturers or retailers but instead saw themselves as intermediaries. The author who had once dealt directly with the printer was now required to do so through the publisher. Large publishing houses rapidly became divided into editorial, production, promotion, and distribution departments, and ranks and hierarchies quickly developed within these divisions. The post of editor was created largely to insulate the other departments from authors and their demands. Publishers, at the top of the hierarchy, gained dignity and status by removing themselves from the inkstains of the printshop, the blue pencil of the editor, and the cashbox of the bookseller.

Walter Hines Page, in his volume *A Publisher's Confession* (1905), repeatedly used the word *professional* to refer to publishers. "It is a personal service that the publisher does for the author," wrote Page, "almost as personal a service as the physician does for his patient, or the lawyer for his client. It is not merely a commercial service."[13] Henry Holt, though reluctant to claim full professional status for the publisher, did agree with

---

13. *A Publisher's Confession* (New York: Doubleday, Page and Co., 1905), p. 68.

Page that "there certainly are features of publishing which rise to a professional dignity."[14] And George Haven Putnam used an unmistakably fiduciary tone when he wrote that his ideal authors were those "fully ready to confide to their publishing friends the business interests connected with their literary work."[15]

Publishing in America in the decades since 1900 has come to resemble the true professions in several ways. There is still no formal training program through which a prospective publisher must pass and no license that must be acquired to practice, but trade publishing has become highly departmentalized, and elaborate hierarchies of rank and status have developed within the industry. The various professional associations to which publishers have belonged have had no power to expel persons for misconduct, but they still have exercised some influence on the trade. Relationships between publishers and authors have come to be fiduciary, almost identical on the face of things to dealings between physicians and patients or lawyers and clients. Even experienced authors are usually uninformed about the mechanics of book production, and they often know almost nothing about the marketing aspects of the industry or about the various ways a publisher can promote and distribute a book. Most publishers have preferred that authors be kept *in statu pupillari*. If the publisher (like the attorney or surgeon) possesses the vocabulary and the knowledge of the trade, then the author (like the client or patient) will have no choice but to trust the publisher implicitly. This has been especially true for young authors or for those whose previous books have not sold well.

The author's disadvantage in dealing with the publisher gave rise to another intermediary in America—the literary agent. The first true agents appeared in New York during the early 1890s, and initially they were resented and attacked by established trade publishers. Both Charles Scribner and Henry Holt, for example, felt that an agent destroyed the amicable relationship necessary between an author and a publisher, and each man for a time refused to publish any author who approached him through an agent. Other publishers were less rigid, though most of them still disliked dealing with agents. The agent survived, however, and gradually came to fulfill some of the functions of a labor union for the author. Agents became intermediaries between writers and publishers:

---

14. "The Commercialization of Literature," *Atlantic Monthly* 96 (Nov. 1905): 577.
15. George Haven Putnam and J. Bishop Putnam, *Authors and Publishers*, "7th ed." (New York: Putnam, 1897), p. 142.

they knew the trade and the vocabulary more thoroughly than authors, and they could be tougher, less emotional negotiators, particularly if they represented other writers in whom a publisher was interested.

Ideally, the agent was the author's ally. Ironically, though, American agents became increasingly professionalized after World War I, insulating themselves from authors in a number of ways. Theoretically agents were free to enlighten authors about the book business, but most agents, like most publishers, chose to keep their clients more or less uninformed. And many authors, perversely, chose to stay that way. Literary agents established their own trade associations, and they insisted on being called "authors' representatives" rather than "agents." Ann Watkins, a leading agent during the 1930s and 1940s, ended her 1941 Bowker Lecture with the prediction that literary agents would someday have to be professionally certified in order to work. Watkins found the idea attractive: "The day will come, and soon I hope, when agents will be licensed by the government," she wrote. "I trust I may live long enough to point with pride to a framed certificate—License Number One—which will hang, I promise you, in the most conspicuous place on my office wall."[16] The agent today insists on a fiduciary relationship with the author: often the author is not allowed to participate in negotiations with the publisher, and some agents prefer that there be no contact at all between author and publisher, even in the preparation of manuscript setting copy. Under such circumstances, the author's loyalty is owed entirely to the agent, and the publishing house becomes an impersonal manufacturer and distributor of literary goods.

Writers are at their most productive when they have cooperative and savvy publishers who understand the mechanisms of the literary marketplace, keep them solvent, and get their writings to the public. Such situations have not often existed for serious literary authors in twentieth-century America, however, and the increasing professionalization of American life, particularly of publishers and agents, has been partly at fault. By taking on the trappings of professionalism, publishers and agents have isolated the author from the processes by which writing is made into literary merchandise.

The professions developed in nineteenth-century America more or less contemporaneously with the rise of science and technology. Not coincidentally, this was when American writers began to lose their sense of au-

16. "Literature for Sale," in *Bowker Lectures on Book Publishing* (New York: Bowker, 1957), p. 113.

thority and audience, to retreat from society and to see themselves as alienated, misunderstood figures. This self-image has been carried by authors into the twentieth century. Writers have seemed to provide no utilitarian service, to fulfill no recognized function. They have attempted, and still attempt, to justify their calling by claiming a transcendent contact with a higher truth or perhaps a role as imaginative interpreter of the subconscious mind, but few of their fellow citizens have taken that claim seriously or have even been able to understand it. Part of the problem has been lack of public identity: authors were left behind when the American middle class professionalized itself, and the business conditions under which they have worked since 1900 have been anachronistic.

These conditions have naturally affected the incomes of writers. The emoluments of literary authorship have remained irregular and, on average, quite low. As recently as 1979, the median American author (in one important survey) earned approximately $4,775 annually from writing. Forty-six percent of the authors surveyed held other jobs in order to make ends meet. Authors who had won literary awards or prizes earned, on average, no more than those who had not; writers who had been born into relatively high socioeconomic classes or had been educated in colleges and universities had no higher earnings than those from lower classes or those with less extensive educational training. Fully one-fourth of the authors surveyed had yearly earnings of less than $1,000 from writing.[17]

Authorship in America has not been a profession during this century, nor has it been a trade. It has been more nearly a craft, a cottage industry. The author has crafted literary piecework at home and has carried it to the publisher, who has turned it into salable goods. On a more idealistic level, authorship has been a *vocatio* or calling—a position to which the author has felt summoned, a walk of life the author has had to follow in spite of practical considerations. In cold economic terms, however, authors have been common laborers. Even authors who have earned large sums of money have been, like the lowest-ranking members of the work force, unprotected and for the most part unorganized. Authorship in twentieth-century America has conferred neither high nor low social

17. Paul William Kingston and Jonathan R. Cole, *The Wages of Writing: Per Word, Per Piece, or Perhaps* (New York: Columbia University Press, 1986), pp. 5–9 and passim. The survey was commissioned by the Authors Guild and carried out by the Center for the Social Sciences at Columbia University.

status, and it has been risky financially. Recognition, if it has come at all, often has come late in the author's career or has only arrived after the author's death. Many authors have proved themselves ingenious and adaptable, surviving and producing despite these disadvantages, and walking the line between art and commerce with great skill and success; but they have done so without protection through professionalization or unionization from the forces of a free-enterprise economy.

Chapter 2

Publishing

> A publisher ought, in short, to harness contradictory quali-
> ties by gambling patiently.
>
> —William Jovanovich (1964)

Book publishing, in America and elsewhere, is different from ordinary business. In this chapter we shall examine some of the characteristics that make it distinctive and that affect the author's ability to earn money from writing. These characteristics include the great variety of the product, the relation of new titles to the backlist, the necessity of cross-subsidization within large houses, the balance between fixed costs and running costs, the importance of the advance, and the struggle for price maintenance.

The chief factor that makes book publishing distinctive from other business is the enormous variety of its product. "A book is a thing by itself," wrote Henry Holt. "There is nothing like it, as one shoe is like another, or as one kind of whiskey is like another. Intelligent book buyers want *that* book; no other will fill its place."[1] Because books are specialized, varied merchandise, they are difficult to market. Certain products, such as foodstuffs, are sold to practically the entire general public, but the novice publisher quickly learns that there is no single "general reading public," despite what book critics and literary historians might think. Instead there are many small publics for the printed word, some of which overlap, and all of which must be approached by different marketing and distribution strategies.

The typical American trade publisher during this century has offered a great variety of books to the consumer. By no means all of that offering has been literary or belletristic. Publishers' lists have contained popular history, memoirs, biography, travel books, social commentary, and much other nonfiction. Educational, technical, and specialist books have often been predictable sellers, as have cookbooks, how-to-do-it books, and technical manuals—all devised for specific markets and often written by authors to whom publishers have assigned these topics. Some publishers

---

1. "The Commercialization of Literature," *Atlantic Monthly* 96 (Nov. 1905): 596.

have established separate divisions for children's books and religious titles; others have specialized in textbooks and reference works, which can yield predictable sales over long periods of time.

In a large American trade firm, these various types of books have usually been published under the same imprint, or under a group of related imprints, but the books have really been issued by small, separate units within the parent company, each one of which has had its own editorial, production, and promotion staffs. These small publishing units have shared distribution arrangements and have been financially interrelated, but in most respects they have been self-contained business units, loosely bound together within the larger company. Until fairly recently, British and Continental publishing did not follow this pattern, and it is still not so widespread in Europe as it is in America. The typical publishing operation there has in the past resembled a small to midsized business; the typical American trade house, by contrast, has more nearly resembled a department store.

An important feature of publishing that has also distinguished it from most other businesses is the backlist. Until fairly recently, a high percentage of a trade publisher's earnings came from the backlist, and it was in the publisher's best interest to build a recognizable and consistently profitable line of titles that would sell steadily over the long term. Once a backlist was established, in fact, it was difficult for the publisher to change its character or the image of the firm that the backlist had created. A strong backlist protected the publisher during slow seasons or economic recessions. In fact, the publisher could cut back on new titles or cease new publishing altogether and simply manage, or "milk," the backlist. Most American trade publishers before 1950 attempted to strike a balance between new titles and backlist staples. If the backlist were allowed to become overly large and the volumes did not sell with sufficient rapidity, then too much capital was tied up in stock and too much cash eaten up by warehousing. In such cases, the publisher eventually faced a crisis in liquidity. On the other hand, if most of the titles on the current list sold out in the short run, then the publisher had no dependable backlist to generate operating expenses or venture capital and had to continue to issue quick sellers. Most publishers therefore learned to give some attention to less volatile types of publishing in order to stay in business.

A good example of a twentieth-century American publisher who did *not* pay close attention to his backlist was Horace Liveright, who had good publishing instincts but who disliked the mundane side of the book trade. Liveright combined with Charles and Albert Boni in 1917 to form the firm of Boni and Liveright. Their most valuable property, in the pre-paperback days of 1917, was the Modern Library, a reprint series that had developed from the Little Leather Library, a Boni venture. Properly managed, as the major part of the backlist, the Modern Library could have been the underpinning of Liveright's entire publishing enterprise, but he neglected the series, preferring instead to gamble on potential best-sellers. As a result Liveright was several times forced to rescue the firm from near-bankruptcy by selling off partnerships to ambitious young men like Bennett Cerf and Donald Friede. Liveright was also lucky and did have several best-sellers—Gertrude Atherton's *Black Oxen,* Hendrik Van Loon's *The Story of Mankind,* Samuel Hopkins Adams's *Flaming Youth,* and Anita Loos's *Gentlemen Prefer Blondes.*

Liveright liked to gamble, not only in publishing but also on Broadway productions and the stock market, and his chronic need of cash eventually caused him to sell off the Modern Library to Cerf and his friend Donald Klopfer in 1925 for two hundred thousand dollars. Liveright continued to devote most of his attention to speculative publishing and by 1929 had again brought his firm to the brink of insolvency. This time he was forced to give up control of the business to Arthur Pell, who attempted to institute fiscal reforms but was unsuccessful. In 1933 the publishing house, unable to recover from many years of financial mismanagement and now lacking the Modern Library as a safety net, went into receivership.[2]

Cerf learned from Liveright's example, and when he and Klopfer formed their publishing partnership in 1925, they decided to spend their first few years in refurbishing the Modern Library and building up a nationwide distribution network. By 1932 they had begun to call their operation Random House and had branched out into the production of limited editions. At about this time they also began to publish full-length new books by living authors. The Modern Library had in effect become

2. An excellent biographical treatment is Walker Gilmer, *Horace Liveright: Publisher of the Twenties* (New York: David Lewis, 1970); see also "Liveright, Seltzer, and the Bonis," in Charles A. Madison, *Book Publishing in America* (New York: McGraw-Hill, 1966), pp. 330–38. On the Modern Library, see Gordon B. Neavill, "The Modern Library Series and American Cultural Life," *Journal of Library History* 16 (Spring 1981): 241–52, and "The Modern Library Series: Format and Design, 1917–1977," *Printing History* 1 (1979): 26–37.

their backlist, and they had built up a considerable fund of venture capital. Cerf and Klopfer signed Eugene O'Neill and Robinson Jeffers from Liveright when that firm failed, and they became Faulkner's publishers three years later when Random House annexed the Smith and Haas list, but they only took on these authors after the Modern Library had put them on solid financial footing. Unlike Liveright, Cerf and Klopfer learned early in the game that attention to the backlist was necessary if one were to survive in publishing.[3]

What kind of publisher is best for a serious literary author? A venturesome gambler, a relentless merchandiser, or a conservative backlist-builder? There is no single answer. Authors and publishers often come together by chance; sometimes an author is dissatisfied with a previous house, or the new house is rumored to be the "right" kind of firm. Most of the matches are imperfect, but occasionally an author does find an entirely compatible publisher. For example, a nearly perfect author-publisher relationship from the period covered in this study is the one between Alfred A. Knopf and H. L. Mencken. Knopf issued a relatively small list of titles, kept his advertising dignified in tone, and published physically attractive books. Because his overhead and promotion expenses were low, he was able to reach the break-even point on books like Mencken's at around two thousand copies. That was fortunate, because Mencken's works, though widely reviewed and frequently attacked, did not sell in great quantities. They did, however, enjoy long runs and usually proved to be good backlist titles, selling in moderate numbers year after year. The only Mencken volume that made a genuinely strong showing at the bookshops was *Treatise on the Gods,* the first edition of which appeared in 1930, thirteen years after Knopf had begun to publish his work. Mencken was genuinely surprised. Two weeks after publication, Blanche Knopf wrote him: "I wish we had bet on the sale of *Treatise on the Gods.* You were sure we would not reach five thousand. Well we have sold five thousand sixty-eight copies to date."[4] Reading through the surviving Mencken-Knopf correspondence, one senses that HLM was satisfied with relatively small numerical sales. He would surely have been

3. *At Random: The Reminiscences of Bennett Cerf* (New York: Random House, 1977), pp. 44–67; Madison, *Book Publishing in America,* pp. 356–60, 507–10.

4. Blanche Knopf to Mencken, 17 March 1930, Manuscripts Division, New York Public Library, quoted in Mary Miller Vass and James L. W. West III, "The Composition and Revision of Mencken's *Treatise on the Gods,*" *Papers of the Bibliographical Society of America* 77 (4th Qtr., 1983): 454.

less comfortable with Liveright, for example, or with an aggressive, sales-minded firm like Doubleday.

Mencken's friend Sinclair Lewis, however, moved to Doubleday in 1931 for precisely that reason—because Nelson Doubleday, son of the founder, Frank Doubleday, was known to be a vigorous merchandiser of literary wares. When Lewis became a Doubleday author, he already had several best-sellers to his credit, and most observers in the trade predicted great success for the partnership. Lewis had his eyes open: he had been courted by numerous other houses but had opted for Doubleday because of its large size and strong business stance. As Lewis wrote to a disappointed suitor at Viking, "My decision is based on what is equally their fault and virtue—their vast organization and list."[5] But Lewis gradually became disenchanted with Doubleday's methods over the next nine years. What he missed was personal attention from the publisher. In 1940 he decided to take his books elsewhere, and on 12 September of that year he wrote "an affectionate but definite letter of farewell" to Nelson Doubleday. In the letter Lewis complained, "You have not the slightest interest in me, nor in my novels as anything more than items on your sales list. . . . I'm just sorry that you have found sales-promotion more fun than traditional publishing."[6]

Ellen Glasgow had left Doubleday six years earlier for similar reasons. She had moved to Alfred Harcourt (Lewis's former publisher), who had been wooing her since 1929 and whose publishing philosophy was different from Doubleday's. Harcourt used various enticements in 1929, including his "small and carefully selected list." He also promised to give "special publishing attention" to Glasgow's novels.[7] She turned him down in 1929, but he kept in contact with her and in August 1934 persuaded her to come over to his house. Harcourt played on the fact that his firm was based in New York City. The Doubleday publishing enterprise had been founded in New York in 1897, but in 1910 Frank Doubleday had moved the entire operation to Garden City on Long Island. "I think you are going to decide that you want a New York publisher," wrote Harcourt to Glasgow while she was still making up her mind. "This town is now the center of American publishing to a degree

5. Lewis to B. W. Huebsch, 30 March 1931, Sinclair Lewis Papers, Beinecke Library, Yale University, New Haven, Conn.

6. Lewis Papers.

7. Harcourt to Glasgow, 1 November 1929, Glasgow Papers, Alderman Library, University of Virginia, Charlottesville, Va.

that was not true twenty or thirty years ago. This is not only true as to the mere output of books, but it is true as to reviewing, selling, and the general atmosphere of activity, which means so much in sales."[8] Doubleday, for his part, continued to handle Glasgow's earlier novels, but try as he might he could not please the sensitive author. In 1944 he wrote her: "I hope some day you will live long enough to write me just a plain friendly letter without a complaint!"[9]

Should one conclude that a small, attentive publishing house is best for a serious literary author? In practice this is sometimes not the case. For example, Sherwood Anderson's reputation and income undoubtedly suffered from the fact that he remained for many years with the small firm operated by Benjamin Huebsch. Literary judgment and genial goodwill were Huebsch's long suits, but his marketing system was antiquated. British publisher Frederic Warburg wrote of Huebsch: "He belonged undoubtedly to the horse-and-buggy era of American publishing, a sort of one-man firm, writing his letters longhand, his own editor, production manager, and advertising executive, who actually went out into New York himself to sell copies of his new publications to the booksellers."[10] Anderson's best books sank quickly into obscurity on the Huebsch list, and many New York authors and publishers were puzzled by his loyalty to Huebsch. In late February 1925, Scribners editor Maxwell Perkins attended a luncheon given in Anderson's honor by Huebsch and later wrote about the event to Charles Scribner, Jr. Perkins reported that Hendrik Van Loon, also in attendance, had risen at the luncheon and asked an embarrassing question: "'Why did Mr. Anderson have Mr. Huebsch for a publisher?' . . . This was apparently some sort of a Dutch idea of humor," continued Perkins, "but it was too apt a question by far."[11]

What Perkins knew—indeed, what all publishers from Huebsch to Harcourt to Doubleday knew—was that publishing, like any capitalistic enterprise, is a form of gambling. Publishers risk money on every title, and in the great majority of cases they lose. G. B. Shaw understood the

8. Harcourt to Glasgow, 2 August 1934, Glasgow Papers.

9. Doubleday to Glasgow, 28 September 1944, Glasgow Papers. For a sketch of Nelson Doubleday's career in publishing, see "Doubleday, Doran & Co.," *Fortune Magazine,* February 1936, pp. 73–77ff.

10. Warburg, *All Authors Are Equal* (London: Hutchinson, 1973), p. 123.

11. Perkins to Charles Scribner, Jr., 24 February 1925, Scribner Archive, Manuscripts Division, Princeton University Library, Princeton, N.J.

equation perfectly: "Publishing is not ordinary trade," he wrote. "It is gambling. The publisher bets the cost of manufacturing, advertising and circulating a book, plus the overhead of his establishment, against every book he publishes exactly as a turf bookmaker bets against every horse in the race. The author, with his one book, is an owner backing his favorite at the best odds he can get from the competing publishers. Both are gamblers." [12]

The economics of publishing are such, however, that one best-selling volume, or even a strong seller, can recoup the losses on several other books. Publishers can thus cross-subsidize titles on their lists or even cross-subsidize departments within their houses. (Usually it is serious fiction, poetry, and belles lettres that are so supported.) This situation exists because of the relationship between fixed costs and running costs in the publishing industry. Fixed costs, sometimes called "plant" costs, occur before the book goes to press. These are charges for editorial work, design, typesetting, proofing, artwork, and printing plates (either offset or relief). Usually they do not recur. Running costs, by contrast, are those that the publisher must pay every time new copies of a title are ordered—paper, ink, binding, dust jacket, makeready, press time, and shipping. Except for massive printings of popular fiction or for multicolor art books, running costs are almost always much lower per copy than fixed costs, and the profit margin on impressions subsequent to the first is consequently higher. While a strong-selling book is still in its initial trade run, its price does not alter; the publisher therefore realizes a profit after a book sells past its break-even point, a point that has risen steadily, for a typical American trade book, from about 1,250 or 1,500 copies in 1915 to 3,000 in 1950 to perhaps 4,500 or 5,000 today for small houses and as high as 10,000 for large publishing operations. These shifts in the publishing equation have been caused by steadily rising costs for printing, advertising, distribution, and overhead.

Higher margins of profit on later printings originally were made possible during the 1830s, when stereotype plating began to be employed in the American publishing industry. With the text cast in metal plates that could be stored between impressions, the publisher could avoid the expense and bother of resetting type every time more copies were needed. The introduction of more durable electrotype plates later in the nine-

12. Shaw, "Sixty Years in Business as an Author," *The Author* 15 (Summer 1945); quoted from its appearance in *American Mercury* 62 (Jan. 1946): 35.

teenth century and the advent, during this century, of flexographic plates (made of plastic or rubber) and offset plates (flat sheets of metal that pick up or repel ink by chemical processes) has made plating of one kind or another so common that it is almost unheard of today to print a trade book from standing type.[13] Once these technological advances had become established, the challenge for the publisher became knowing when to reprint a title and in what quantity. Every reprinting was also a reinvestment, a gamble; the possible losses were lower, but no publisher wanted to be caught with too much back stock of a title, especially if the book were not a candidate for the backlist.

A good example of conservative gambling on a book was the strategy employed by Scribners in reprinting F. Scott Fitzgerald's popular first novel, *This Side of Paradise,* in 1920. The book was widely praised (and widely damned) for the picture Fitzgerald had painted of his postwar generation in America. Demand for copies was heavy through the summer and fall of 1920, and Scribners could have ordered two or three very large impressions and attempted to flood bookstores with copies. The firm, however, elected to play safe, apparently fearing that the success of *This Side of Paradise* was faddish and temporary and that demand for the book would vanish as quickly as it had arisen. If that happened, Scribners could be left with a large stock of unsold copies. Accordingly Scribners issued eleven successive small reprintings in runs varying from two thousand to five thousand copies and waited for each impression to sell nearly out before ordering another. Undoubtedly Scribners lost some sales (and Fitzgerald lost some money) as a result, and the firm surely spent more by incurring makeready costs for eleven reprintings rather than for two or three. Scribners, however, did not lose its major profits on the book in a final, large, unsold impression.[14]

That is almost exactly what *had* happened to George H. Doran the previous year with Daisy Ashford's *The Young Visiters,* a mystery story supposedly written by a nine-year-old British girl and incorporating her errors in orthography and grammar, as the misspelled title suggests. Doran had issued an initial printing of only five thousand copies, but once the rumor got about that the actual author of the book was J. M.

13. For a brief survey of the history of plating, see Philip Gaskell, *A New Introduction to Bibliography,* corrected ed. (New York: Oxford University Press, 1974), pp. 201–6.

14. James L. W. West III, *The Making of* This Side of Paradise (Philadelphia: University of Pennsylvania Press, 1983), pp. 111–15.

Barrie, it became an overnight success. Doran overreacted. Years later he recorded the story in his memoirs: "As quickly as printers and binders could manufacture, we produced exactly 250,000 copies. We sold 200,000, and at this point a fickle public decided to have no more of it and the sale ceased with the abruptness of a guillotine decapitation. Finally the ten-cent stores slowly disposed of what was left."[15]

The relationship between fixed and running costs explains why certain secondary publishers could issue cheap reprints of books, either in cloth or paper bindings, from the original plates. Cheap hardcover reprints before 1950—in such series as the Dollar Book Club, A. L. Burt, Blue Ribbon Books, and Grosset and Dunlap—could be sold for a fraction of the price of the original trade edition because only running costs were involved, and these could be further reduced by using inexpensive paper and binding materials, which the reprint publisher could buy in quantity. Reprint publishers also employed long press runs (usually a minimum of ten thousand copies) in order to incur makeready expenses only once.

Fixed and running costs also had an effect on authors' royalties. Escalation clauses in publishing contracts (10 percent on the first twenty-five hundred copies sold, 12.5 percent on the next five thousand copies, 15 percent thereafter—or some such variation) were made possible by the increased profit margin on reprintings subsequent to the first. Copies sold before the book broke even often yielded a higher percentage of the gross income to the author than to the publisher, but copies sold after the break-even point were more profitable for the publisher. This arrangement was justified by publishers on the grounds that they had used their own capital to finance the original manufacture of the book and would need risk capital in the future to publish other books. The profit margin on cheap reprints, however, was not so large as it was on trade reprints, so the author here was usually asked to accept a lower royalty, often a straight 10 percent, or even a flat fee. Sometimes, for a work of doubtful sales appeal, a certain number of copies would be held exempt from royalty (perhaps the first one thousand) so that the publisher would have a better chance to recoup the initial investment. For enormously popular works, however, an author might command a straight 20 percent royalty

15. Doran, *Chronicles of Barabbas, 1884–1934* (London: Methuen, 1935), p. 160. It is ironic, by the way, that *This Side of Paradise*, which was peppered with errors in spelling and grammar, was several times compared by book reviewers to *The Young Visiters*. Fitzgerald, to his chagrin, found himself being referred to as "the Princeton Daisy Ashford."

from the first copy sold, as George Barr McCutcheon did with Dodd, Mead and Company.[16]

Another important figure in the book-publishing equation was the advance. For many years this was simply an early payment against expected royalties; once the book had earned royalties past the point of the advance, the author would begin to receive further payments in cash. Before 1950 a typical advance or series of advances on which the author might subsist while working on a manuscript might total no more than five thousand dollars and was often less than that. In recent years, however, advances have gone much higher, and it has become the norm to treat them as nonreturnable flat fees. In today's literary marketplace these are called "guarantees," and most authors prefer them over traditional advances, especially for leased paperback rights. Publishers, by contrast, dislike paying large advances, particularly on unwritten work, because these advances tie up capital for long periods of time. For their part, authors can object (as John O'Hara frequently did to Bennett Cerf) that the publisher's practice of paying royalties only once or at most twice a year allows the publisher to keep the author's money for many months— to draw interest on that money or use it to launch other books while the author waits for payment. "As matters now stand," wrote the irritable O'Hara to Cerf, "Random House is getting rich on my money, and I am *not* getting rich on my money. Your wife and sons will get and are getting the benefit of my work, but my wife and my daughter are not."[17]

Publishers have always wanted to control the number of books that are published, but it has been much easier to produce books in America during this century than it has been to sell them, and many publishers have succumbed to the temptation of overproduction, hoping that one winner would cover the losses on the other titles. Most observers of the American book trade, including O. H. Cheney, who published an extensive and valuable survey of the domestic publishing industry in 1931, have agreed that far too many titles have been published annually in this country.[18] These observers have also agreed that there is no easy way to make pub-

16. McCutcheon's literary ledger, listing details of his publishing contracts, is at the Beinecke Library, Yale University, New Haven, Conn.

17. O'Hara to Cerf, 25 February 1961, *Selected Letters of John O'Hara*, ed. Matthew J. Bruccoli (New York: Random House, 1978), p. 359; also see O'Hara to Cerf, 14 December 1964, p. 467.

18. *Economic Survey of the Book Industry, 1930–1931* (National Association of Book Publishers, 1931; reprint, New York: Bowker, 1960), esp. pp. 84–89.

lishers cut back. No publishing house would be willing to give up to a watchdog agency its right to publish more than a fixed number of titles in a given season. Almost the only time such reductions worked was during World War II, when paper shortages forced publishers to reduce their output. Not surprisingly, the war years were quite successful for U.S. publishers. Virtually everything they produced sold well, and they weathered the paper restrictions easily.

A related problem has been price maintenance. The most bitter fights in American publishing history have come over price-cutting and loss-leadering—first during the 1840s with piratical paperback publishers, later in the 1890s with J. W. Lovell's "book trust" of cheap reprinters, and again in the early 1900s between Macy's department store and established New York publishers. In order to survive, trade firms have had to establish a loose monopoly—a difficult thing to do in publishing. British book publishers were able to do it in 1899 when they passed the Net Book Agreement, a cooperative arrangement by which they agreed not to supply books at trade discount to booksellers who sold them below the publisher's net price. Underselling had plagued the British industry for decades: it had caused price wars among bookshop owners, had interrupted cash flow, and had made account collection difficult. The Net Book Agreement kept booksellers in line; it was a disciplinary measure designed to punish them if they did not uphold the price structure. British publishers, led by Sir Frederick Macmillan, cooperated admirably in establishing the Net Book Agreement in 1899, and they fought off several subsequent challenges to the measure. Especially gratifying to them was their victory in the Times Book War of 1905–7, in which they forced the Times Book Club to cease selling slightly used stock at lower than net prices. The Net Book Agreement became the "Magna Carta" of the book trade in Great Britain during the twentieth century, making it much simpler for houses there to maintain a conservative, backlist-oriented style of publishing.

The major trade publishers in America attempted to emulate the British by announcing in March 1901 their own Net Book Agreement, a measure virtually identical to the one adopted by the British. Macy's department store in New York, however, challenged the agreement in 1902 by suing the American Publishers Association and the American Booksellers Association jointly for restraint of trade and for monopolistic and conspiratorial practices. Macy's lost in the lower courts but persisted; the suits and countersuits dragged through the state and federal courts over the next decade and were finally settled against the publishers. The U.S. Supreme Court held in 1913 that publishers were not exempt from the Sherman Anti-Trust Act and assessed them $140,000 in damages, a heavy blow that resulted in the dissolution of their organization. This court ruling was a turning point in the history of the American book trade. Publishers realized that they would not be able to follow in the footsteps of the British but would instead have to develop a wider-open, less elitist approach to the book business. This has in fact happened in the United States during this century but not without some difficulty, and, as we shall see in the final chapter of this book, not without mixed effects on the careers of serious literary authors.

These various factors—the backlist, cross-subsidization, fixed and running costs, the advance, and price maintenance—have had a daily influence on the operations of publishing houses, on their business strategies, and on the methods they have used in handling their authors. Other matters, not discussed here, have also been of great importance: developments in printing technology, changes in postal regulations, variations in customs laws, and shifts in international copyright agreements. Each of these factors has influenced some phase of the publishing industry, and all of them have combined to influence the business philosophies of individual houses or, in a larger and more general way, of particular literary periods. Authors, in turn, have been strongly affected by these factors, because it has been on the book-publishing business that they have relied for income, and for the dissemination of their ideas.[19]

19. Readers interested in more detailed information about the workings of the publishing industry should consult the three standard histories of the American trade: Hellmut Lehmann-Haupt, in collab. with Lawrence C. Wroth and Rollo G. Silver, *The Book in America: A History of the Making and Selling of Books in the United States,* 2d ed. (New York: Bowker, 1951); Madison, *Book Publishing in America;* and John Tebbel, *A History of Book Publishing in the United States,* 4 vols. (New York: Bowker, 1972–81). Histories of the British book trade include F. A. Mumby and Ian Norrie, *Publishing and Bookselling* (London: Cape, 1974) and Marjorie Plant, *The English Book Trade: An Economic History of the Making and Sale of Books,* 3d ed. (London: Allen and Unwin, 1974). A good overview of the publishing business is Stanley Unwin's *The Truth about Publishing,* issued originally by Allen and Unwin in 1926 and in revised editions in 1946, 1960, and 1976. The 1926 and 1946 editions are the most useful. A comparable book on American publishing is George Haven Putnam and J. Bishop Putnam, *Authors and Publishers,* especially the "7th edition" issued by Putnam in 1897. Good recent books on publishing include, for Great Britain, J. A. Sutherland, *Fiction and the Fiction Industry* (London: Athlone Press, 1978) and, for America, Lewis A. Coser, Charles Kadushin, and Walter W. Powell, *Books: The Culture and Commerce of Publishing* (New York: Basic Books, 1982).

Chapter 3

Distribution

> Even temperately conducted, the miscellaneous publishing
> business . . . is an extremely hazardous business. A hazard-
> ous business must select its risks carefully, and therefore
> cannot successfully be a large one, relative to its rate of pos-
> sible profit. At its wisest, it must be a small business with
> large margins for profits.
>
> —Henry Holt (1905)

The chief problem for the publisher of clothbound books in America
during this century has been lack of an adequate distribution system. Because nineteenth-century American publishers did not establish a nationwide system of marketing, twentieth-century publishers and authors
have functioned at a disadvantage in business. Two of the most important innovations in book distribution during this century—paperbacks
and book clubs—were initiated during the twenties and thirties because
trade publishers could not exploit the national market through conventional means. Both new methods tapped into modes of distribution that
had already been established. Paperback publishers used the existing network for magazine distribution; book clubs used the services of the U.S.
mail.[1] But neither of these methods would have been so successful had
nineteenth- and early twentieth-century publishers been able to build an
efficient distribution system for their books. The reasons for their failure
to do so are tied in with the cultural development of the United States
and with the business history of the country after 1850.

Just as American writers took their first notions about authorship from
the British, so American publishers (as soon as they were financially able,
around the middle of the nineteenth century) sought to model themselves after their counterparts in Great Britain. Intellectually the United
States was still very much tied to Britain throughout most of the nine-

1. For an account of the founding and subsequent success of the Book-of-the-Month
Club, see Charles Lee, *The Hidden Public: The Story of the Book-of-the-Month Club* (Garden
City, N.Y.: Doubleday, 1958). Also see Joan Shelley Rubin, "Self, Culture, and Self-Culture
in Modern America: The Early History of the Book-of-the-Month Club," *Journal of Ameri-
can History* 71 (1985): 782–806. A good history of American paperback publishing is
Frank L. Schick, *The Paperbound Book in America* (New York: Bowker, 1958).

teenth century, and it is no surprise that in publishing—as in philosophy, education, and politics—we patterned ourselves after British or Continental models. Europeans typically saw American publishers as commercially minded buccaneers who made their profits by pirating the works of well-known European authors, particularly British authors. Established American trade publishers were keen to rid themselves of this image and to do business in the manner of the great British and Continental publishers. "Courtesy of the trade"—an arrangement by which an American publisher paid a flat fee to a British author for the exclusive right to publish that author's work in the United States, and by which other American publishers kept away from that author—was in part a practical method of reducing competition and maintaining prices, but it was even more an effort by the American publisher to show the British publisher that he could behave in a gentlemanly fashion.[2]

As early as the 1840s, American publishers regularly traveled to London once or twice a year to make business arrangements with English publishers and to be entertained by them. American publishers enjoyed these jaunts to the intellectual homeland; the memoirs of such major nineteenth-century U.S. publishers as James T. Fields and George P. Putnam are filled with anecdotes gathered on these visits, during which they met and talked business with the prominent publishers of London—Richard Bentley, Frederick and Maurice Macmillan, William Heinemann, John Murray (the younger), George Smith, Sampson Low, John Blackwood, William Longman, and others—and during which they also met famous British authors whose works they would shortly undertake to publish.[3] There was no doubt about relative position and influence: British publishers enjoyed superiority over their American brethren because their houses were older, their backlists stronger, and their images more distinguished. It was American publishers who came to England in search of British books to publish and in hopes of persuading the British publisher to take on some of their own titles. Rarely did a London publisher visit America for the same purposes.

2. Hellmut Lehmann-Haupt, in collab. with Lawrence C. Wroth and Rollo G. Silver, *The Book in America: A History of the Making and Selling of Books in the United States,* 2d ed. (New York: Bowker, 1951), pp. 208–11; Henry Holt, "Competition," *Atlantic Monthly* 102 (Oct. 1908): 522–24.

3. George H. Putnam, *George P. Putnam: A Memoir* (New York and London: Putnam, 1912), esp. the early chapters dealing with Putnam's years on Paternoster Row, 1841–47; James T. Fields, *Yesterdays with Authors* (Boston: Osgood, 1872), esp. chaps. 2, 4, 5, and 7.

American publishers were not entirely subordinate, however. They serviced a large and potentially profitable market, and British readers, curious about American democracy and social practices, were willing to buy some of the books being offered to London houses. Many of these American publishers were men of cultivation and wide experience; cordial and even strong friendships grew up between American publishers and British publishers and authors. George H. Putnam was friendly with the Macmillans, for example, as was Henry Holt. Fletcher Harper and Sampson Low were on good terms, and Frank Doubleday developed firm friendships with both William Heinemann and Rudyard Kipling.

In this situation it was natural for American publishers to borrow many of their business practices from British models. The classic early pattern for a British publisher was that of European publishing generally before 1850. The publisher concentrated on a small field, or group of related fields, and published for a geographically limited and demographically similar market. Annual lists were small and selective; lines of predictable sellers like technical manuals, reference books, textbooks, or religious titles were the underpinning of the house—the publications that subsidized occasional gambles on fiction or poetry. Advertising was limited and conservative in tone; overhead was low. A substantial proportion of sales came from the backlist, and many editorial decisions hinged on how well a title might be expected to perform over the long term.

This pattern of publishing was admirably suited to Great Britain and Europe, where markets were defined by language barriers and were geographically concentrated. Both Germany and France, for example, had national clearinghouses for book distribution. The German one, called the Börsenverein der deutschen Buchhändler, was a marvelous machine for selling books and was the envy of British publishers, as was, to a lesser extent, the French operation, known as La Maison du Livre. Even without a comparable national clearinghouse, British publishers did not do badly at the business of book distribution. Transportation and communication systems there, even during the first half of the nineteenth century, were reasonably well developed, and there was a network of established bookshops that handled distribution. Because almost no one attempted to address a truly mass market, book prices stayed high until late in the century. And when price-cutting became a serious problem, British publishers banded together, secured the cooperation of the Society of Authors, and passed the Net Book Agreement.

These are sound business practices in any field: producing a limited quantity of goods for a well-defined, predictable consumer group; selling those goods for a high unit price, which is maintained by cooperation; conserving profits by avoiding unnecessary overhead, pointless advertising, or far-flung distribution; concentrating on proven products of high quality that will continue to sell year after year; and, above all, not trying to recover an investment too quickly.

But this conservative model of publishing, so well suited to British and Continental conditions before 1850, was not the ideal pattern for the mid- to late nineteenth-century American publisher to follow. Transportation and communication systems in the United States were not yet well developed, reading tastes and education levels were quite varied, there was no effective national network of book outlets, and the industry was full of pirates and price-cutters. Moreover, the public served by an American house was geographically dispersed. As late as 1897, George H. Putnam could still write:

> It costs on an average not less than $10.00 a day to keep a traveller going east of the Rocky Mountains, and in the territory west of the Rocky Mountains the expenses may easily mount up to $15.00 a day. While, in Great Britain, a day's railroad journey will bring a traveller within reach of three or four towns where he may properly expect to find customers, in various districts of the Southern and Western States a traveller may spend an entire day in the journey to a single town, and if, when the traveller arrives, the bookseller happens to be absent or to be in a bad temper, it may be necessary to take the backward journey on the same line, thus spending twenty-four or thirty-six hours' time and "mileage" with absolutely no result.[4]

For these reasons, it was impossible for American publishers to apply the British pattern successfully to the United States as a whole. They therefore did the next best thing and set about creating, artificially, the conditions they needed. Most American publishers learned to concentrate first on their home cities—New York, Philadelphia, Boston—and on a few nearby areas that could be reached easily over established shipping routes. The early nineteenth-century publishers were primarily interested in servicing the urban Northeast; later, when turnpikes, canals, and railroads opened the midwestern states in the 1830s and 1840s, publishers gave attention to cities like Cincinnati and St. Louis, and, through jobbers, to the Midwest generally, but they did not operate in too large a

---

4. George Haven Putnam and J. Bishop Putnam, *Authors and Publishers*, "7th ed." (New York: Putnam, 1897), pp. 195–96.

field. Traveling salesmen could do some business in rural areas and in the South, but the net gain there was usually small. Publisher Mathew Carey and book agent Parson Weems attempted to reach the South, but their success was limited. Areas of high population density were better, more predictable for the publisher.[5]

The efforts of Ticknor and Fields to reach book buyers in the Old Northwest and the South during the mid-nineteenth century can perhaps be taken as typical for the trade as a whole. The firm began doing business as a book-publishing house in 1832 and at first sold most of its output locally in Boston. After 1840, however, Ticknor and Fields stepped up efforts to distribute books to the Northwest and South, relying on retail booksellers rather than on traveling book agents or subscription lists. The firm met with some success, especially in the Northwest, but the record of its dealings with booksellers in such cities as Cincinnati, Richmond, and New Orleans is filled with wrangles over discount systems, account collection, and the returns policy. W. S. Tryon, who along with William Charvat did pioneering research on the cost books of Ticknor and Fields, concluded that by 1850 two conditions had become imperative for success in book publishing: "an urban community of sufficient proportions to warrant the existence of bookstores; and an adequate transportation system by which the issues of the publishing house could reach the bookseller."[6] Neither existed for the country as a whole.

Established American publishers of the mid- to late nineteenth century thus found it necessary to create, for business purposes, what was in effect their own European country—the urban Northeast. It was risky to invest large amounts of money in an attempt to reach a wider market: potential book buyers were undeniably out there, but the publisher had to be careful not to be seduced by the lure of high numerical sales. It is quite possible, in business, to sell many more units of merchandise than one's competitors but to net much less money. Far-flung markets must be serviced by a sales force, higher shipping charges must be paid, advertis-

5. William Charvat, "Publishing Centers," in *Literary Publishing in America, 1790–1850* (Philadelphia: University of Pennsylvania Press, 1959), pp. 17–37; also James Gilreath, "Mason Weems, Mathew Carey and the Southern Booktrade, 1794–1810," *Publishing History* 10 (1981): 27–49.

6. "The Publications of Ticknor and Fields in the South, 1840–1865," *Journal of Southern History* 14 (Aug. 1948): 319. Also see Tryon's "Ticknor and Fields' Publications in the Old Northwest, 1840–1860," *Mississippi Valley Historical Review* 34 (Mar. 1948): 589–610; and "Book Distribution in Mid-Nineteenth Century America," *Papers of the Bibliographical Society of America* 41 (1947): 210–30.

ing expenditures must be increased, accounts must be collected. Prudent American publishers such as the Putnams, Appletons, and Scribners therefore chose, for the most part, to stay on familiar regional turf, and the consequences for American cultural and intellectual development were profound.

The obvious solution would have been for the United States to develop a system of regional publishing, and to some degree that is what happened in Chicago, Cincinnati, Indianapolis, and other midwestern cities. But these midwestern publishers, with the exception of two or three houses in Chicago, were conservative and never attempted much in the way of original literary publishing. The bulk of their publishing was religious, instructional, and utilitarian, though they did do a brisk business in reprints and in pirated British titles.[7] The South did not support strong book-publishing houses; its antebellum economy was predominantly agrarian, its population largely rural, and its transportation routes poorly developed and maintained. In 1857 the *American Publishers' Circular* listed more than three hundred publishers in the United States, but of these, fewer than thirty were in the South, and of those, half were located in Baltimore.[8] There were a good many local printer-publishers in the South, and they issued numerous titles, but they lacked even the rudiments of a distribution system. Books published in North Carolina, for example, seldom reached readers even in the adjacent states of Virginia and South Carolina. The Civil War wiped out investment capital that might have backed southern publishers after 1870, and in any case overland shipping routes had been wrecked by the war. By the time the South recovered economically, northeastern publishers had become so firmly established, so solidly a part of the post–Civil War northern plutocracy, that there seems never to have been a serious effort to challenge them.[9] A network of bookshops was never built up in the South or the West, and habits of book buying and book ownership never became strong among

7. See Walter Sutton, *The Western Book Trade: Cincinnati as a Nineteenth-Century Publishing and Book-Trade Center* (Columbus: Ohio State University Press, 1961), esp. pp. 18–29 and chaps. 9, 10, 16, and 19; see also the sketches of the various midwestern houses in Charles A. Madison, *Book Publishing in America* (New York: McGraw-Hill, 1966) and John Tebbel, *A History of Book Publishing in the United States,* 4 vols. (New York: Bowker, 1972–81).

8. Tryon, "Ticknor and Fields in the South," p. 305.

9. Jay B. Hubbell, *The South in American Literature, 1607–1900* (Durham, N.C.: Duke University Press, 1954), pp. 214–15, 363–66, 454–55, 712–13; also Michael O'Brien's introduction to *All Clever Men, Who Make Their Way: Critical Discourse in the Old South* (Fayetteville: University of Arkansas Press, 1982), esp. pp. 5–8.

middle-class citizens in either region. The Far West, in particular, was not nearly well enough settled to support book publishers or bookshops until well into the twentieth century. As a result of these factors, an effective system of regional publishing or a truly efficient network of book distribution has never been developed in America.

The history of the publishing industry in the United States has been closely related to the commercial development of the entire nation. Early publishers were hampered by a lack of capital, by the absence of strong copyright laws (which, in effect, would have granted a monopoly on a literary work to a single producer, thereby making price maintenance feasible), by poor internal transportation routes, and by high freight rates. From about 1800 until 1830, it cost the exorbitant sum of fifteen cents per ton per mile to ship goods by turnpike; publishers were unable to reach the Midwest under such conditions and still make a profit. Canal rates from around 1815 to 1860 were more reasonable—about 2.3 cents per ton per mile—and publishers took advantage of those rates to stock canal boats with books in the spring and fall and send them off to midwestern consumers.[10] The South remained difficult of access: most turnpikes and railroads ran east to west, as did the Erie Canal and most other man-made waterways. Southern markets usually had to be reached by ocean-going vessels that moved along the coast from northeastern harbors to major ports such as Richmond, Charleston, Savannah, Mobile, and New Orleans, where there were bookshops. Lippincott and Mathew Carey did some business in this fashion, but because the southern population was predominantly agrarian, it was usually necessary also to send out traveling booksellers.

American business leaders of all types were cautious about expanding their markets before 1850. Most did not have access to the capital required to open up new sales territories, and the population still was so small and scattered in relation to the size of the country—twenty-five million citizens in 1850—that nearly all heads of firms had to be prudent. Most were unsure about how to proceed. Their biggest worry was price control, and they spent most of their energies attempting to deal with upstart competitors in territories that had already been developed.[11] This was es-

10. Keith L. Bryant, Jr., and Henry C. Dethloff, *A History of American Business* (Englewood Cliffs, N.J.: Prentice-Hall, 1983), pp. 94–95, 101; William Charvat, *The Profession of Authorship in America, 1800–1870* (Columbus: Ohio State University Press, 1968), pp. 35–36.

11. Thomas C. Cochran, *Business in American Life: A History* (New York: McGraw-Hill, 1972), pp. 61–72, 152–53.

pecially true in publishing. Cheap paperback (or "yellowback") firms saw that there were new readers to be serviced in the Midwest and South and in the Northeast as well. Twice (in the 1840s and again in the 1880s and 1890s) they seized the main chance and attempted to reach these buyers through wildcat paperback publishing—pirated titles, cheap materials, long press runs, low prices, and nontraditional outlets. Nearly all of the established trade publishers in New York and Philadelphia decided not to compete with these price-cutters; only the Harpers and, later, the Appletons tried to issue lines of cheap books as competition for the speculators. The other houses simply waited for paperback publishers to kill off one another or be ruined by one of the periodic depressions that plagued the U.S. economy. Paperback firms, they reasoned, would not have enough working capital or a large enough margin of profit to survive bad economic times. That is, in fact, what happened. But there was an important side effect: experienced trade publishers, who could have worked up new territories in the South and Midwest in a slower, more responsible fashion, were discouraged from doing so. There seems to have taken root in the minds of most nineteenth-century American publishers a disinclination to conduct business on a national scale. Northeastern publishers came to treat outlying U.S. markets much as British publishers treated their colonial market—as a secondary area in which one had to be careful not to lose one's shirt.

It must be said that before about 1850, advanced printing technology was not widely enough available to allow eastern publishers to manufacture copies cheaply enough or in sufficient quantity to go after nationwide markets. With certain exceptions, most notably the Harpers, book publishers were not especially interested in developing new printing methods; most were content to limit their territories and to follow conservative, time-tested business strategies. It was the highly competitive American newspaper and periodical publishers who brought in new technology and, indirectly, forced book publishers to abandon their old habits. Publishers began to experiment with power-driven presses in the 1820s. (The very first ones were driven by horses, but after 1830 Isaac Adams's steam press dominated the market.)[12] Just as important was the development of the cylinder press in the 1830s; early models used cylinders both for inking and impression, and around 1847 printers succeeded

12. Ralph Green, "Early American Power Printing Presses," *Studies in Bibliography* 4 (1951–52): 143–53.

in getting the type off the flat bed of the press and onto the curved cylinder. Machines to make paper in rolls, not sheets, had been developed in England as early as 1800 and were in general use in the United States by the 1830s. The first commercial typesetting machines were ready by the mid-1850s, though they needed refinement. Power-driven paper folders and case-binders were also being developed at about this time, and stereotyping and electrotyping were becoming fairly common. These developments did not come about simultaneously. One development necessitated others: presses became better and faster, cylindrical papermakers had to be built to feed the presses, and typesetting equipment had to catch up.[13]

Traditional book publishers were not eager to adopt this new technology because it meant entering into wider, more competitive markets, and, of necessity, called for concentration more on short-term than long-term profits. Many publishers saw these developments as departures from an ideal of publishing that they (or in some cases their fathers) had adopted from the British. Thus, publishing during the late 1800s and early 1900s can be seen as a struggle, in the traditional publisher's mind, between old and new. Many new publishing houses were beginning to do business in the manner of other American firms, seeking high profit and exploiting a growing technology and an expanding market, but older publishers continued to think of their calling—their "profession"—in terms taken from an earlier time. One sees these tensions especially in the writings of George H. Putnam, Henry Holt, and Walter Hines Page, all of whom were leaders in the industry.[14]

These same forces operated on the author. Trained to see authorship as something less than a legitimate occupation, an author nevertheless could not fail to recognize that a publisher, if so inclined, could now reach a numerically larger and geographically more widespread audience than before. How to appeal to that audience, how to reach those readers! These became new challenges for many American authors.

In truth, conditions were not ideal for book publishing in the United States during the mid- to late nineteenth century. They were almost per-

13. Lehmann-Haupt, *The Book in America,* pp. 142–47.
14. Putnam and Putnam, *Authors and Publishers,* and George H. Putnam, *Memories of a Publisher* (New York and London: Putnam, 1915); Henry Holt, "The Commercialization of Literature," *Atlantic Monthly* 96 (Nov. 1905); idem, "The Commercialization of Literature: A Summing Up," *Putnam's Monthly* 2 (Feb. 1907); [Walter Hines Page], *A Publisher's Confession* (New York: Doubleday, Page and Co., 1905).

fectly suited, however, for newspaper and periodical publishing, which tends to flourish in countries that are large, politically active, and economically vigorous. The newspaper and magazine industries took the lead in American publishing; the book industry followed behind, both economically and philosophically. Left alone, the traditional American trade publisher before 1900 would probably have preferred to follow British models, limit output, curtail the market, control prices, and stay out of publishing on a national scale.

Faced with this kind of conservatism, American authors learned to look to magazines and newspapers for steady income and wide exposure. The European model of book publishing works well for an author in a traditionally minded, aristocratic society in which there are numerous (if not especially generous) sources of private, institutional, or governmental patronage. In a free-enterprise democracy, however, one needs an active, aggressive, profitable publishing industry in order to support a class of literary authors. Reputable northeastern book publishers during the second half of the nineteenth century saw themselves as part of the urban elite; they seem to have been most comfortable with authors who conformed to the European pattern—who had independent means or who worked at other occupations. In some major houses, that attitude persisted until well into the twentieth century. Scribners, for example, was much better able to deal financially with Henry James, Theodore Roosevelt, Willard Huntington Wright (S. S. Van Dine), Christian Gauss, and Douglas Southall Freeman—all of whom either had independent means or worked at other occupations—than with authors like F. Scott Fitzgerald and Thomas Wolfe, both of whom lived entirely on literary earnings.

In the early 1900s, a new kind of book publisher with a new philosophy of publishing began to operate in the American literary marketplace. These publishers brought many ideas over from newspaper and magazine publishing, and they had the advantage of the 1891 international copyright agreement. Traditional nineteenth-century book publishers, British and American, were essentially passive. They waited for authors and manuscripts to come to them, and they accepted or rejected books according to how well those books would fit in with the rest of the list and the character of the house. There was little stratification or departmentalization in the typical publishing operation. Everyone did a little of everything—editorial work, production, promotion, and distribution. When railroads and other modes of transportation began to open up a true national market for other consumer goods in America, however, new people came into publishing and brought with them fresh ideas about how to market literary wares. Frank Doubleday, Edward Bok, and S. S. McClure developed a more active and aggressive role for the publisher after 1900. Instead of waiting for authors to come to them with manuscripts and ideas, these new publishers themselves became the originators of ideas that they would assign to proven writers. Doubleday, in particular, saw that the creative process in book publishing could be reversed. He believed that the publisher should "invent books which the public really wants, or thinks it wants" and then engage writers to create those books for public sale. Much of the famous muckraking journalism of the early 1900s was created in just this way.[15]

Novelist Frank Norris, who worked for Doubleday as a manuscript reader and literary adviser, had seen this reversal of the creative process at first hand:

> At present the stimulus to, and even the manner of, production of very much of American fiction is in the hands of the publishers. No one not intimately associated with any one of the larger, more important "houses" can have any idea of the influence of the publisher upon latter-day fiction. More novels are written—practically—to order than the public has any notion of. The publisher again and again picks out the man (one speaks, of course, of the younger generation), suggests the theme, and exercises, in a sense, all the functions of instructor during the period of composition. In the matter of this "picking out of the man" it is rather curious to note a very radical change that has come about in the last five years. Time was when the publisher waited for the unknown writer to come to him with his manuscript. But of late the Unknown has so frequently developed, under exploitation and by direct solicitation of the publisher, into a "money-making proposition" of such formidable proportions that there is hardly a publishing house that does not now hunt him out with all the resources at its command.[16]

Along with this new publishing style came a greater emphasis on departmentalization and hierarchy in the normal trade house. Such developments were typical of American business generally in the early decades of the twentieth century, a period during which big business came to

15. Frank Doubleday, "The Young Publisher's Chances," *Publishers' Weekly,* 19 September 1903, p. 452. See also chap. 3, "International Copyright and the Emergence of Progressive Publishing," in Christopher P. Wilson, *The Labor of Words: Literary Professionalism in the Progressive Era* (Athens: University of Georgia Press, 1985), esp. pp. 74–82.

16. "Salt and Sincerity," in *The Responsibilities of the Novelist* (New York: Doubleday, Page, 1903), p. 258.

dominate life in the United States. The demand for cheapness, utility, and wide circulation, together with the lure of a vast domestic market (features noticed by analysts of American culture since Tocqueville), had their effect on the publishing industry and eventually produced, in the late 1930s, the first successful experiment in paperback publishing in this country, Robert de Graff's Pocket Books. Doubleday, however, had identified the challenge as early as 1903: "How to sell the book—the single volume: novel, history, biography, or what not—to any really large proportion of the people who would buy if they knew of its existence is what the publisher wants to know." Doubleday himself experimented with several marketing strategies, including subscription books, and, later, book clubs; but he realized that "there remain to be invented a good many ways of bringing the book and the reader together."[17]

Publishing boomed after World War I, just as most other American businesses and industries did. Many of the old firms—Scribners, Holt, Putnam, and Lippincott—remained strong, but most of the exciting publishing during the 1920s and 1930s was done by new houses that grew up during that period. Alfred A. Knopf, Random House, Viking Press (which took over the B. W. Huebsch list), Simon and Schuster, and Boni and Liveright (later Horace Liveright) were the most visible firms of the time. All were more willing to address large markets than were the older houses, although some of these new firms, as they succeeded, began to take on the conservative habits of the older publishers. A powerful inducement to do so, of course, was the Great Depression. In the past, general economic depression had always meant hard times for American publishing. The depression of 1893–97 had been particularly difficult for trade houses. During those earlier depressions, publishers had sometimes made the mistake of overproducing in an effort to stimulate the market. This time most American publishers cut back on titles and stuck to predictable kinds of publishing or lived off their backlists and reprint lines. The only major publisher to fail was Liveright. World War II was a good time for publishers, and most of them entered the 1950s in strong financial condition. Ironically, however, their success did not inspire them to establish a truly national market or a nationwide distribution system for clothbound books. Publishing had become so urban-centered that national marketing seemed out of the question.

17. "The Young Publisher's Chances," p. 452.

The second half of the twentieth century and the first several decades of the twenty-first may turn out to be the period in the history of American publishing when the industry finally disperses over the entire country and sets up regional publishing firms and distribution systems. The ease of communication afforded by the telephone and the attractiveness of relatively low overhead in cities outside New York have already enticed several publishers to other locations. If such a system of regional publishing and distribution is indeed established, its effect on American authors will be far-reaching. They will have to change their conceptions of their potential audiences, reconsider their material, and perhaps rethink their ideas about themselves. It is doubtful that a true profession of authorship will grow up, but strong regionally based publishing can only help authors in the pursuit of their craft, their calling.

Chapter 4

The Editor

> Don't pass judgment on a manuscript *as it is,* but *as it can be made to be.*
>
> —M. Lincoln Schuster (1962)

American publishing houses did not always employ editors. Before the 1880s there was usually little division of responsibility within a trade house; the operation was small by modern standards, and the tasks that one associates with editing were performed by the publisher. Indeed the word *editor* derives from the Latin verb *ēdĕre,* which means "to put forth, give out, publish." The French word *éditeur* still carries that meaning, as does the English noun *edition.*

Editors began to be designated in trade publishing houses during the late nineteenth century when American firms began to be divided into departments. Many of these first editors—William Brownell, Richard Watson Gilder, Edward L. Burlingame, and Henry Mills Alden, for example—were also magazine editors, and they carried their titles with them into book publishing. The post of editor was created to relieve the publisher of duties that had become overly demanding. The editor was a good example of Thorstein Veblen's "middle man," functioning as an extension of the publisher's mind and style and serving as a buffer between publisher and author. The book trade had gradually become more lucrative and financially more stable, but in the process it had also become more complicated. The publisher was now an overseer, a business manager whose time was mostly spent watching the balance sheet and representing the house to the public. Separate departments for production, promotion, and distribution were created, and accountants were hired to keep track of collections and cash flow. The publisher had less time than ever, and probably less inclination, to deal with authors and their manuscripts. The editor took over these duties.

Some nineteenth-century publishing houses had allowed one partner to be responsible for authors, leaving the other partner or partners free to attend to business matters. James T. Fields of Ticknor and Fields dealt with authors; his partners handled most business matters. Fletcher

Harper usually represented his firm to authors, and his three brothers performed other tasks. Samuel Appleton, head of the house, preferred to assign authors to his son William Worthen. Such arrangements persisted into the twentieth century; Frank Doubleday, of Doubleday, Page and Company, left dealings with all but a few authors to his junior partner Walter Hines Page, for example. Horace Liveright took a hand in the editing of Theodore Dreiser's writings in the 1920s, and as late as the 1950s Alfred Knopf was functioning as John Updike's editor, but those two arrangements were atypical for their times. Usually such publisher-author relationships occurred only when editors had risen through the ranks to become partners in publishing houses or had broken free to begin their own firms. In such cases, these publishers would continue to edit the writings of their prize authors in order to retain their loyalty.

Typical of the first generation of editors in American publishing houses was Henry Mills Alden of Harper and Brothers. Alden, a native of Vermont, had worked as a child laborer in the textile mills but had risen through his own industry to take degrees at Ball Seminary (1853), Williams (1857), and Andover Theological (1860). He pursued the ministry for a short time but had a weak voice and decided not to be ordained. He came to New York City in 1861, with but two dollars in his pocket, to seek his fortune. Through Harriet Beecher Stowe, whom he had known at Andover, he made contact with James Russell Lowell, James T. Fields, and Wendell Phillips; he contributed a few pieces to the *Atlantic* and in 1863 landed an editorial position at Harper and Brothers on *Harper's Pictorial History of the Great Rebellion*. He settled at Harpers and stayed there for more than fifty years, as managing editor of *Harper's Weekly* until 1869 and thereafter as editor of *Harper's Magazine* until his death in 1919.[1]

Like many editors in publishing houses of this period, Alden worked on both magazines and books. Book publishing and magazine publishing were more closely allied then than they are today, and Alden moved easily between the two. He had a nineteenth-century sense of the editor's role as cultural arbiter and protector of public standards. He was circumspect about the new realism and was strongly opposed, toward the end of

1. Alden appears to have been a company man. In the Harper papers at the Pierpont Morgan Library, New York City, is a letter to the directors, dated 31 December 1880, in which Alden asks for his first raise in ten years. He has earned seventy-five dollars per week since 1871; he requests a higher salary in order to be able to send his daughter to a "first class school."

his life, to most of the literary experimentalism he observed. He had little tolerance for the depiction of unvarnished evil in fiction: "Shadows have their place in the brightest picture," he admitted, but "authors who revel in brutalities, who enjoy an infernal habitation not for its purgatorial fires but for its sulphurous airs . . . do not come within the scope of the demand of any species of human culture."[2] It is perhaps not surprising that Alden discouraged Dreiser from submitting the manuscript of *Sister Carrie* to Harpers in 1900.[3]

Alden published three books during his lifetime—*God in His World* (1890), *A Study of Death* (1895), and *Magazine Writing and the New Literature* (1908). This last, by title, appears promising, but one searches the volume in vain for a clear statement of editorial practice or for a glimpse of the workings of the House of Harper. The advice to authors is elevated, circumlocutory, and almost entirely lacking in specificity. One presumes that Alden offered concrete criticisms to authors from his editorial desk at Harpers, but if he was a typical editor of the period, he did not enter into the creative process. His primary function, as he saw it, was the maintenance of standards.

The career of William Crary Brownell, an editor at Scribners, was in many respects similar to Alden's. Brownell was descended from early New England settlers and spent his childhood and adolescence in New York City and Buffalo. He entered Amherst in 1867, at the age of sixteen, and after graduating became a reporter and later the city editor for the New York *World*. From 1879 to 1881 he served on the staff of the *Nation;* after marriage and a three-year residence in Paris with his wife, he returned to America and worked for the *Philadelphia Press* for four years. In 1888 he joined Charles Scribner's Sons and eventually became a fixture there, serving as editor and literary adviser for forty years until his death in 1928. Brownell, a Democrat and an Episcopalian, was one of the most conservative literary and cultural critics of his day. He produced a series of volumes in the tradition of Sainte-Beuve and Matthew Arnold; today he is sometimes linked with the New Humanists Irving Babbitt, Paul Elmer More, and Stuart Sherman. Brownell had little sympathy for the avant-garde and inveighed against their "spirit of revolt—conceived, of

---

2. *Magazine Writing and the New Literature* (New York: Harpers, 1908), p. 68.
3. See the historical commentary for the Pennsylvania Edition of *Sister Carrie* (Philadelphia: University of Pennsylvania Press, 1981), p. 519.

course, as renovation by its votaries, but still manifestly in the destructive stage, witnessed by the fierceness of its iconoclastic zest, so much greater than its constructive concentration."[4]

Brownell worked with most of the important Scribner authors of the 1890s and early 1900s; probably his greatest achievement as editor was to encourage and guide Edith Wharton during the early and middle years of her career. Wharton in turn judged him "the most discerning literary critic of our day" and praised his ability to "exercise the subtlest critical function of detecting differences where most observers see only a resemblance." For her, he was at his best in "sounding the springs of human character."[5] She saw him rarely; indeed, nearly the whole of their relationship was epistolary. From beginning to end she addressed him as "Mr. Brownell"; his letters to her (inscribed in the elegant hand taught him as a child by P. R. Spencer, originator of Spencerian penmanship) all begin "My dear Mrs. Wharton." Reading through his letters to her today (they are preserved in the Scribner Archive at Princeton University), one finds remarks that are helpful, restrained, and impartial—but rarely specific.

Brownell's letters of declination to authors were masterpieces of indirection. Thus the following to a Miss Pusey in 1898:

> We have been extremely interested by your novel "Society" and in finally coming to the conclusion that we shall be unable to undertake its publication we beg you to believe that we do so very regretfully & for reasons which by no means impeach the many excellences of the book. Your own statement that it is not a first effort was not needed to convince us that it is the work of a practiced hand and we cannot too warmly congratulate you on many of its felicities of literary expression and really dramatic situation. If we may venture to make the suggestion, however, we think you will agree with us that the public taste of the day, rightly or wrongly, has concluded it to be the wiser course to demand observation rather than imagination of all authors of whom the strenuous personality is not already eminent or overmastering. . . .

And so on. Only in reader reports meant for internal circulation at Scribners did Brownell exhibit much personality. Here is a portion of his as-

4. "Standards," *Proceedings of the American Academy of Arts and Letters and of the National Institute of Arts and Letters,* no. 10 (1917). For information about Brownell's career, see Gertrude Hall Brownell, ed., *William Crary Brownell: An Anthology of His Writings together with Notes and Impressions of Later Years* (New York: Scribners, 1933) and Me Tsung Kaung Tang, "William Crary Brownell, Literary Adviser" (Ph.D. diss., University of Pennsylvania, 1946).

5. Wharton, "William C. Brownell," *Scribner's Magazine* 84 (Nov. 1928): 596.

sessment of Henry James's *The Sacred Fount* after it was submitted to the firm:

> It is surely the n + 1st power of Jamesiness. . . . I have had the greatest difficulty in following it—indeed I couldn't follow some of it. . . . It gets decidedly on one's nerves. It is like trying to make out page after page of illegible writing. The sense of effort becomes acutely exasperating. Your spine curls up, your hair-roots prickle & you want to get up and walk around the block. There is no story—oh! but none at all. That is the *point* no doubt. It is a *tour-de-force;* as if James had said "You don't like my psychology & hair-splitting & analysis and no melodrama, eh! Well I will carry it all the farther for your opposition.[6]

But to the authors themselves Brownell seldom offered more than general advice. Certainly he did not meddle with their manuscripts. "I don't believe much in tinkering," he wrote Wharton, "and I am not *suffisant* enough to think the publisher can contribute much by counselling modifications."[7]

Ripley Hitchcock, an approximate contemporary of Brownell's and Alden's, was one of the first American trade editors to take a more active role in working with the manuscripts of his authors. Hitchcock's background was similar to Alden's and Brownell's. Like the former he was a New Englander, and like the latter he entered the world of letters through newspaper work. Hitchcock was a native of Fitchburg, Massachusetts; his father was a prominent physician, publicist, and author, and his mother was for a time a professor of Latin at Mount Holyoke. After an undistinguished career at Harvard (A.B. 1877), Hitchcock moved into newspaper work and by 1882 was art critic for the *New York Tribune.* During the summers of 1882 and 1883 he traveled extensively in the West, the Northwest, and Mexico; among his papers at Columbia University is a photograph of him standing by a campfire, in pith helmet and puttees, with a revolver strapped around his waist. By 1890 Hitchcock had left newspaper work to become editor and literary adviser at D. Appleton and Company. In 1902 (two years after the Appleton bankruptcy) he departed from that firm and in 1903 began work as vice-president at A. S. Barnes and Company, a house that specialized in school texts. This arrangement endured only some three years, however, and in 1906 he be-

6. The letter to Miss Pusey and the reader report on James are both quoted in Roger Burlingame's history of Charles Scribner's Sons, *Of Making Many Books* (New York: Scribners, 1946), pp. 68–69, 36–37.

7. Quoted in R. W. B. Lewis, *Edith Wharton* (New York: Harper and Row, 1975), p. 133.

came an editor at Harper and Brothers (which was still recovering from its own 1900 bankruptcy). There he remained until his death in 1918.[8]

During his twenty-eight years in book publishing, Hitchcock worked with many authors. He served as editor for Woodrow Wilson and John Jacob Astor, Hall Caine and Zane Grey, Joel Chandler Harris and Richard Henry Stoddard, A. C. Doyle and Rudyard Kipling, Frank R. Stockton and Gilbert Parker. His editorial labors were expended on such diverse projects as Wilson's *A History of the American People,* Stephen Crane's *The Red Badge of Courage,* Dreiser's *Jennie Gerhardt,* Stoddard's *Recollections,* Astor's *A Journey in Other Worlds,* Mrs. Clarke Pyrnelle's *Miss Li'l Tweetty,* and Dr. Arthur N. Davis's *The Kaiser as I Knew Him* (a memoir by Kaiser Bill's dentist). Hitchcock specialized in the creation and management of books in series: his most successful such venture at Appleton was the "Story of the West" series. Among his papers is a folder of series ideas for Harpers, including prospectuses for lines of books on "Correct Speaking and Writing," "Good Health for Girls," and "Hints for Mothers."

In personality Hitchcock was courtly, reserved, cautious, and refined. He was unusually patriotic and deeply religious. After his death, his pastor at Grace Episcopal Church in New York City spoke of "how deep and real his faith was, expressing itself daily in acts far beyond any deeds springing from a more conventional belief." Another eulogist recalled that Hitchcock had "used a sensitive religious instinct in securing from brethren in his craft many books of the higher life."[9] Among the religious writers whose works Hitchcock edited were Hamilton Wright Mabie, long-time editor of the *Outlook,* and Hezekiah Butterworth, author of *The Story of the Psalms* and *David, the Shepherd Boy.*

Hitchcock was himself a writer of some note. His earliest interest was art, and he was especially knowledgeable about etchings. Later he published books on other subjects: these volumes included *Thomas De Quincey* (1899), *The Louisiana Purchase* (1903), *The Lewis and Clark Expedition* (1905), and *Decisive Battles of America* (1909). He was an early inductee into the National Institute of Arts and Letters and eventually became secretary of that body. He was a prominent member of both the Authors

8. For information about Hitchcock's career I have relied on the sketch of him in the *Dictionary of American Biography;* on entries in various Harvard class reports for 1902, 1917, and 1927; and on information in the folder of biographical data in the Hitchcock Papers, Columbia University, New York.

9. Obituary folder, Hitchcock Papers.

Club and the Century Club and was on close terms with William Dean Howells and other authors of equal stature. Near the end of his life he served, for two consecutive years, as one of the judges for the new Pulitzer Prize in biography.

The novel for which Hitchcock was best known as editor was the phenomenally successful *David Harum,* by Edward Noyes Westcott, first published by Appleton in 1898. Hitchcock transformed *David Harum* from a disorganized and unpublishable manuscript to one of the most famous best-sellers in the history of late nineteenth- and early twentieth-century American literature. The story is worth retelling for the light it sheds on Hitchcock and for what it tells about the transformation in trade-house editing during this period. Westcott, a banker from Syracuse, New York, was afflicted with chronic tuberculosis. He was forced by illness to take an extended leave from work, and during that period he wrote *David Harum,* a novel set in upstate New York. The manuscript was rejected by several publishers before it came to Hitchcock at Appleton in December 1897. Hitchcock recognized that the best scenes involving the most attractive character, the shrewd cracker-barrel philosopher David Harum, were buried near the middle of the manuscript and were all but overwhelmed, in the narrative as a whole, by a saccharine love plot. With Westcott's permission, Hitchcock transferred five chapters from the center of the manuscript to the beginning, cut and tightened the love story, and revised the entire manuscript for style and narrative pace. Hitchcock's most important alteration was to transfer a clever and memorable horse-swapping scene from the middle of the book to the beginning.[10]

David Harum was published by Appleton in September 1898 (Westcott, unfortunately, had died the previous March), and the novel was an immediate hit. During March and April of 1899 it was selling at better than a thousand copies a day. In subsequent years the book developed into a publisher's dream title for the backlist: by February 1904 its sales had reached 727,000 copies; by 1935 it was into its one hundredth trade

10. Hitchcock's work on *David Harum* is described in numerous accounts, but the most reliable appear to be a typewritten account inserted into a copy of the novel in Hitchcock's papers (*David Harum* File 3); an account written by Hitchcock and quoted in an unattributed clipping of a magazine story titled "David Harum" (5 pp.) in a file of publicity materials at Columbia; Clarence Clough Buel, "A Friend's Tribute to Ripley Hitchcock," *New York Times Book Review,* 26 May 1918, p. 248; and Helen Sargent Hitchcock (his widow), "David Harum Philosophizes Again," *New York Times Magazine,* 17 July 1938, pp. 10ff.

printing; by 1946 its sales in hardback were reckoned at 1,190,000—and this on the occasion of the issue of a paperback impression of 241,000 copies. After Appleton sold drama rights for *David Harum* to Charles Frohman, Hitchcock and his wife adapted the novel for the stage and shared box-office receipts equally with Appleton for a three-year run on Broadway and a long series of road performances. The novel was twice adapted for the movies, with Will Rogers in the title role for the second screen incarnation.[11]

David Harum was the book for which Hitchcock was famous in publishing circles. It is also the editing job for which he apparently wanted to be remembered. *David Harum* is mentioned prominently in the obituary tributes to Hitchcock in 1918: Crane's name is sometimes mentioned, but Dreiser's is not. Among Hitchcock's papers at Columbia—papers saved by him and placed there by his widow for a biography that has never been written—there are three full cartons of material on *David Harum*. By contrast there is very little about Dreiser and nothing at all of consequence about Crane.

Of American novels published in the nineteenth century, *David Harum* was one of the two or three most successful, in commercial terms, after *Uncle Tom's Cabin*. The story of Hitchcock's editing of the manuscript was reported in the press at the time of publication and became part of the subsequent lore that gathered around the book. What effect did Hitchcock's success as creator of this silk purse have on editors who were his contemporaries in American publishing? What effect on editors who followed him in the trade? What effect on his own subsequent editing of Dreiser and other authors?

It is impossible to answer these questions with precision. There has been some controversy among scholars recently over the role played by Hitchcock in the editing of Crane's *The Red Badge of Courage* and in the revision and/or expurgation of *Maggie: A Girl of the Streets*. There is no conclusive evidence for assigning responsibility for the changes in *The Red Badge* or *Maggie* to Hitchcock. But in one case at least—Hitchcock's editing of Dreiser's *Jennie Gerhardt*—we do have concrete evidence upon which to comment. Dreiser submitted a ribbon typescript of *Jennie* to Harpers sometime in the early months of 1911; he retained a carbon copy of this text. Harpers accepted *Jennie* for publication, but before it went

11. Frank Luther Mott, *Golden Multitudes* (New York: Macmillan, 1947), pp. 202–3; and "David Harum," the unattributed clipping mentioned in n. 10.

to the compositor Hitchcock and his subeditors subjected the text to a round of heavy cutting and revision. So extensive were their alterations that a fresh typescript had to be prepared for the printers. Dreiser accepted the revisions by Hitchcock and his staff, but we know from his correspondence with H. L. Mencken and from his comments to others that he felt uneasy about the changes.[12] *Jennie Gerhardt* was published and was commercially successful for a serious novel in 1911; Dreiser never attempted in later years to have his original text restored, but he did save the carbon typescript of his uncut and unrevised version. Today it is in the Barrett Collection at the Alderman Library, University of Virginia. Collation of his carbon typescript against the text of the first edition (all other intervening forms between manuscript and print having perished) has revealed changes that are thoroughgoing and profound. Characterization was altered, antireligious sentiment was blunted, and the bleak philosophical naturalism of the book was muted. Dreiser's clumsy but powerful prose was rendered smoother and more conventional. The majority of these changes appear to have been made by (or done under the supervision of) the man who edited *David Harum*. As we shall see, Hitchcock's job on *Jennie Gerhardt* is typical of much that would happen to the texts of important American novels in the decades to follow.[13]

By the 1920s the editor had become the next most powerful person in the typical American trade house, subordinate only to the publisher. From the author's point of view, the editor was even more important than the publisher, who by now was usually a remote figure who could be protected from the author's demands. It was the editor who handled all face-to-face relationships, judged manuscripts, and had them transformed into books. The editor's power was drawn both from above and below. Many of the editor's duties—decisions about contract terms, pursuit and acquisition of manuscripts, building and managing the backlist—were identical to the responsibilities of the old-time publisher. Within the firm, the editor had the crucial responsibility of approving the production schedule and making it dovetail with promotion and sales efforts. And the editor also did much of the mundane work with manuscripts, checking matters of fact and accuracy and, in smaller houses, even copyediting for the compositor.

12. James L. W. West III, "Double Quotes and Double Meanings in *Jennie Gerhardt*," *Dreiser Studies* 18 (Spring 1987): 1–11.
13. This collation was performed as part of the work in progress on the Pennsylvania Edition of *Jennie Gerhardt*.

Besides dealing with manuscripts and authors, the editor had to think three to five years ahead in relation to the backlist and to predict which books would endure in value, continue to sell, and fit into the areas of concentration of the house. A successful editor in a large twentieth-century publishing firm had to know about every phase of the operation. A book designer, by contrast, could function effectively without knowing much about promotion and distribution. What designers did need to know was how a book would be advertised so that they could create the proper look—serious, popular, or something between—and which trim sizes would fit into the company's bulk shipping cartons. Beyond such details, however, the minutiae of how the book would be advertised and distributed or how the receipts would be collected were not the designer's concern. An editor, however, had to be knowledgeable in all of these areas and for that reason often put in an apprenticeship in each wing of the business before settling down to full-time editing. The editor was the lynchpin of the enterprise; the firm and its authors stood or fell according to how well editors performed their tasks.

How did the editor's duties evolve? Initially editors seem to have taken their instructions directly from publishers; only later did they come to function almost independently and to create, within large houses, their own groups of subordinates, their own stables of authors, and their own backlists. Early editors, like Brownell and Alden, were judges of manuscripts; the decision to accept, reject, or send back for revision was theirs. They seldom ventured to offer extensive advice for revision or improvement. Once a manuscript was accepted for publication, an editor checked it for offensive words or libelous statements but rarely suggested cuts or made independent revisions of phrasing. This has always been the attitude of British editors toward their work; trade editors in Great Britain claim not to understand or approve of the more active roles played by their American counterparts. Edward Garnett is the notable exception: he entered into the compositional process with D. H. Lawrence and, to a lesser extent, with Joseph Conrad; but he appears to have been almost unique in early twentieth-century British publishing.

In America, by contrast, the role of the editor after 1920 was defined by Maxwell Perkins. Perkins has been pictured as a genius and a saint, and although he was neither, he was certainly an honest and sensitive man, the best handler of authors in the history of American literature. Nearly all the editors who were his contemporaries and successors in New York publishing attempted to emulate his style, though sometimes with unfortunate results.[14] By all accounts, Perkins could understand what his writers were attempting to do—could virtually assume their personalities and viewpoints—and could offer useful criticism from his assumed position. He was able to sense each author's predicament and to know what advice would help overcome a stumbling block. He was a faithful correspondent and an indefatigable reader of manuscripts. He was also a gentleman, with good manners, and with enough of the eccentric about him to make him intriguing. Perkins, however, was not especially good at the detailed work of editing. He disliked meticulous checking of facts and was a poor speller. Sometimes he had subordinates handle these chores for him; at other times he let them take care of themselves. His first big success—F. Scott Fitzgerald's *This Side of Paradise*—was marred by misspellings and grammatical blunders, and Fitzgerald took a bad licking from the reviewers. Indeed, the reception of *This Side of Paradise* established the tone of Fitzgerald's literary reputation for the rest of his career. To the reviewers he was a muddleheaded pseudointellectual, a glib illiterate who could not spell Samuel Johnson's name correctly.[15]

Perkins did not like to make changes within the sentence. That is, he did not as a rule tamper with the style of his authors. He often suggested cuts, however, and his innately conservative temperament usually made him delete highly emotional or poetic passages, which he referred to as "dithyrambs."[16] He was not always helpful with problems of structure and chronology. Fitzgerald's last complete novel, *Tender Is the Night* (1934), is marred by a confusion in chronology that obscures its time scheme and some of its internal symbolism. Perkins apparently did not notice the problem when he read the manuscript, and it remains in the text today.[17]

14. A. Scott Berg, *Max Perkins: Editor of Genius* (New York: E. P. Dutton, 1978); Malcolm Cowley, "Unshaken Friend" (2 pts.), *New Yorker* 20 (1 and 8 April 1944). For British publisher Victor Gollancz's remarks on American editors and on Perkins specifically, see Sheila Hodges, *Gollancz: The Story of a Publishing House, 1928–1978* (London: Gollancz, 1978), pp. 169–70.

15. James L. W. West III, *The Making of* This Side of Paradise (Philadelphia: University of Pennsylvania Press, 1983), pp. 96–119. For other comments on Perkins as editor, see Burroughs Mitchell, *The Education of an Editor* (Garden City, N.Y.: Doubleday, 1980), p. 32 and passim. Mitchell was Perkins's successor at Scribners.

16. Francis E. Skipp, "*Of Time and the River:* The Final Editing," *Papers of the Bibliographical Society of America* 64 (3d Qtr., 1970): 314–15.

17. Matthew J. Bruccoli, *The Composition of* Tender Is the Night (Pittsburgh: University of Pittsburgh Press, 1963).

Perkins was squeamish about certain subjects. About an incest scene in *Kit Brandon,* Perkins wrote Sherwood Anderson as follows: "I am sending you on a few more galleys, and these involve that part which seems to me so dangerous to the book because of throwing around Kit a kind of horror which the reader could never shake off. . . . It is a hard question, but at least I think that you might be able to cut out in two places a few lines." Anderson, ever agreeable, went along with Perkins. "I am reading the proof," he wrote back, "and I believe I have found the solution of the spot in the story that gave you a rather bad effect. By this new version the thing didn't happen as Kit escaped. I think this handling of it would get away from the fact of the consummation and at the same time explain her running away from home."[18]

Perkins may also have overemphasized fiction when he advised his authors about their careers. Michael S. Reynolds, one of Ernest Hemingway's best recent biographers, has suggested that Perkins did not reinforce Hemingway's desire to be a man of letters in the true sense—a writer not only of novels but of essays, criticism, reviews, and nonfiction as well. Perkins encouraged Hemingway to write only fiction, which was potentially more salable, and in so doing may unknowingly have contributed to the writer's block that plagued the author during the last two decades of his career.[19]

And yet Perkins could often give precisely the right advice at an important point in an author's life. Erskine Caldwell, just beginning his literary career in 1930, was attempting to decide whether to draw on New England material for his novels or to cast his fiction in a southern setting. He sent unpublished short stories of both kinds to Perkins in the spring of 1930, and Perkins urged him to concentrate on the South. The southern stories, Perkins felt, were deeper and less anecdotal than the New England material. Caldwell took Perkins's advice and, in 1931, delivered *Tobacco Road* to Scribners—the first of a series of successful novels by him about the South.[20]

The relationship between Perkins and Conrad Aiken was not so

18. Perkins to Anderson, 25 June 1936, and Anderson to Perkins, 3 July 1936, quoted in John Delaney, "The Archives of Charles Scribner's Sons," *Princeton University Library Chronicle* 46 (Winter 1985): 160.

19. Michael S. Reynolds, "Words Killed, Wounded, Missing in Action," *Hemingway Notes* 6 (Spring 1981): 2–9.

20. Perkins to Caldwell, 2 June 1930, Scribner Archive, Manuscripts Division, Princeton University Library, Princeton, N.J.

smooth. Few things are more difficult for an author than to break with an editor of recognized ability, but if the relationship is uncomfortable, the author must leave. Aiken had looked forward to working with Perkins at Scribners, but during the late 1930s Aiken turned increasingly in his fiction writing to the novella form, and Perkins, who wanted him to write a full-length novel, was not enthusiastic about the shorter works. Aiken was displeased and eventually arranged to move to another publisher— Duell, Sloan, and Pearce. In his last letter to Perkins, Aiken wrote, "I can't help feeling, you know, that ever since Blue Voyage you've had a kind of queer *idée fixe* as to what was to be expected of me—some remote and grandiose notion as to the sort and shape of novel you wanted me to do—and I've felt, with every book since, that your *idée fixe* simply prevented you from seeing anything else."[21] Aiken felt that Perkins and Scribners had allowed his books to come out but had not truly *published* them. Financial returns from his volumes were so small that he had been forced to rely on what he called "the sticky toils of journalism."

But it is doubtful whether any publisher could have handled Aiken's work with much more success than Scribners; Aiken's writing had low commercial potential. According to Perkins, the attitude of the Scribners sales force had finally come to be a factor: "If a publisher brings out a number of an author's books in succession, and they do not sell," he wrote to Aiken, "it is a fact that his selling force gets discouraged and begins to think of the case as hopeless."[22] Perkins did his best to encourage Aiken as long as he was a Scribner author. In a letter to Bernice Baumgarten, Aiken's agent at Brandt and Brandt, Perkins arranged for an escalating royalty on Aiken's book of poetry *Time in the Rock* (1936). According to the terms of the contract, payment would move from 10 percent to 15 percent after three thousand copies had been sold. Perkins did not expect a book of serious verse, even one by Aiken, to sell more than three thousand copies, but he hoped that the contract, with its escalation clause, would not "look so discouraging to Conrad." In the same letter, Perkins admitted to Baumgarten that he no longer even bothered to figure in overhead when running preliminary figures on Aiken's books, so certain was he that they would not break even.[23]

It is tempting to idealize and even romanticize the relationships be-

---

21. Aiken to Perkins, 6 July 1939, Scribner Archive.
22. Perkins to Aiken, 11 December 1939, Scribner Archive.
23. Perkins to Baumgarten, 18 March 1936, Scribner Archive.

tween authors and editors. The editor can easily be seen as a supportive authority figure or, conversely, as an insensitive yahoo. Perkins, for example, has been romanticized almost beyond recognition. He had the good fortune to discover Fitzgerald and, through Fitzgerald, to bring Hemingway into the Scribner fold; later he recognized Thomas Wolfe's talent and helped Wolfe turn his sprawling drafts into two publishable novels. Perkins also worked closely with Marjorie Kinnan Rawlings in the creation of her most famous book, *The Yearling* (1938). He was courtly, handsome, and paternal; his ability to function as a father figure was one of his most valuable assets. Most young writers need the support and assurance of an older authority figure, someone who will affirm the value of devoting one's life to literature. Editors frequently are called upon to serve in this role, and Perkins did it well. He was a brilliant editor, but occasionally he stumbled—especially in matters of detail.

The popular notion of the duties of a modern editor is inaccurate. The amount of time the typical editor in a general trade house was able to spend working with the manuscripts of literary authors usually was small. Fiction, poetry, drama, and belles lettres probably made up only about 10 to 12 percent of the list, and as a group these books nearly always lost money. The generalist editor therefore had to spend a considerable amount of time on cookbooks, how-to-do-it books, technical manuals, religious titles, gardening books, and calendars. Many of the books published by twentieth-century American firms were not even written by the person whose name appeared on the title page. It was common for a firm to contract for the memoirs of a famous public figure or movie star and to pay a large advance on an unwritten manuscript. When the manuscript came in, it was often badly organized and woefully written. It became the duty of the editor to put the book into publishable shape. For decades, editors have been silent collaborators on numerous volumes of popular history, autobiography, travel, and psychological advice. One of the givens that a twentieth-century editor has assumed when drawing up a contract with a prospective author is that the manuscript will almost surely need work. The editor will be the one to do it.

When trade editors take this attitude toward the majority of their manuscripts, it is difficult for them to adopt a hands-off attitude toward the few manuscripts that are creative or literary. Much of what the editor deals with is popular fare in any case—mysteries, historical romances, middlebrow novels—and authors of these books are often not especially sensitive about editorial collaboration. Partly as a result of this kind of thinking, an important psychological principle sometimes comes to operate in an editor's mind: if one holds the title of editor and draws a salary from a publishing house for editing, then one must indeed edit manuscripts, not leave them alone. Editors must justify their positions by making suggestions and changes. Very lightly edited manuscripts can suggest that the editor is not doing a thorough job, and there is always the matter of the book's performance on the market: if it does poorly, the manuscript must not look as if it were cursorily dealt with. Variations of this attitude are common in medicine, law, teaching, military service, government work, and auto repair. The editor is under indirect pressure to alter manuscripts, even when alterations are not necessarily required.

Some authors have been quite difficult for editors to handle. Probably the most troublesome author in the Random House stable during the mid-1930s, for example, was William Saroyan, whose collection *The Daring Young Man on the Flying Trapeze* was published to excellent reviews in 1934. Saroyan frequently sent wires begging for advances on unwritten material and then had the bad judgment simultaneously to approach other publishers about jumping to their houses. (At least one of those publishers, Richard Simon of Simon and Schuster, passed on a quiet word about the matter to his friend Bennett Cerf.) Saroyan also allowed more than one firm to represent him to foreign publishers and, as a result, sold off some foreign rights that he did not in fact possess, much to Cerf's consternation.

Saroyan wanted to make a splash with his second book, *Inhale and Exhale*. He was confident about the manuscript of the collection when he sent it to Cerf in September 1935. "Boy o boy o boy, Bennett: what a book. . . . It's got everything, every God damn thing anybody could want in a book, and a couple of things extra, gratis, to give them their money's worth." Saroyan made his wishes explicit: "Print every word. Follow my arrangement of the stories. . . . I've been working like a bastard, day and night, and night and day. . . . I've edited perfectly, not putting anything in that didn't belong in, and what I'm sending you, on the level, has got to be put in the book." But Saroyan had no experience in the economics of trade publishing, and he had put together a massive manuscript containing "three novels, one travel book, one play, all kinds of stories: great prose, new forms, every kind of horse manure known, and a few unknown kinds."

The Random House editors wrote Saroyan that the manuscript of *Inhale and Exhale* would have to be cut, prompting an emotional response: "I would like to know of any other writer in America who could write so greatly and so poorly in one book," he argued. The title, he explained, was symbolic: "The good goes with the lousy: the living goes with the dying. And also: the bad is not too bad because it is the work of the same man who wrote the good." Saroyan felt that the collection was unified, with a central theme running "right smack straight through the whole book." The economics of the situation, however, were unyielding: even in cut form, Cerf wrote Saroyan, the book would run more than five hundred pages, for which the break-even point would be approximately five thousand copies—"and that doesn't include one cent of overhead." The book almost surely would not sell well enough for Random House to recoup its investment. Saroyan gave in, but with great reluctance. His subsequent letters were chastened and hurt: "Ah Jesus, this is a lousy racket," he wrote Cerf on 26 November. "I used to think all you had to do was write well. Write well? All you need to do is figure out the angles."

The actual editing of the manuscript was painful for Saroyan. He himself had made a mistake about its word count, and this error was compounded by Saxe Commins, a senior editor at Random House. Commins had accepted the author's own estimate of length for the manuscript of *Inhale and Exhale* and had cut 27 of the original 124 items to produce what he assumed was a manuscript of some 175,000 words. But Saroyan's estimate had been wildly off; the printer's castoff of the once-cut manuscript was fully 292,000 words. Commins therefore had to subject *Inhale and Exhale* to a second round of editorial cutting. Saroyan was resigned but histrionic: "Anyhow, I'm through with argument: if you must cut, cut away, and God have mercy on your souls. Frankly, no crime could be more punishable by eternal agony." Unfortunately, there was more to come. The British edition of *Inhale and Exhale,* published by Faber and Faber in 1935, was cut further—and by no less an editor than T. S. Eliot. Saroyan's reaction to Eliot's cuts is not preserved in the Random House files, but he could not have been happy.[24]

Commins is the editor whose name is most frequently mentioned in

24. This correspondence is in the Random House Collection at the Butler Library, Columbia University, New York. The quotations are taken from Saroyan to Cerf, 10 and 12 September 1935, 11 and 26 November 1935; Saroyan to Donald Klopfer, 8 October 1935; Cerf to Saroyan, 22 November 1935.

company with Perkins's. During his twenty years at Random House, Commins edited the work of Eugene O'Neill, William Faulkner, Gertrude Stein, W. H. Auden, John O'Hara, Sinclair Lewis, and Robinson Jeffers. No editor of his time, not even Perkins, dealt with so many important writers. Commins's great strength was his kindness and patience; he was upright, faithful, patriotic, and conscientious. His manner with his authors was calm and reassuring: many of his letters to them begin, "Put your mind at ease." Commins did not have Perkins's gift for recognition of talent—nearly all of his authors came to him with established reputations—but he formed strong relationships with many of them and helped keep their books coming to Random House.

Commins did, however, irritate some authors by his work on their manuscripts. He was a disappointed writer himself: he had been trained as a dentist but had given up that occupation and had gone to Europe in the 1920s to be a writer. His own work was not promising, but in Europe he began a lifelong friendship with O'Neill, for whom he served as typist, courier, and factotum. Partly through O'Neill's influence, Commins got a position in 1930 as editor at Covici-Friede; about a year later he moved to Boni and Liveright to work with O'Neill's books. Horace Liveright's financial irresponsibility had brought that house to the verge of collapse, and O'Neill wanted Commins there as his personal agent and informant. Management of the firm had been taken over by Arthur Pell, but the financial problems were so serious that Pell could only postpone the inevitable failure of the business. By early 1933 Commins could see disaster approaching, and he notified O'Neill, who was in Europe. Pell owed O'Neill a great deal of money in back royalties—money that the playwright would never see if the firm went under. Commins had learned that his employers were temporarily solvent: he knew that their house would collapse if O'Neill left the stable and word of his defection reached other authors to whom Pell owed money. Commins therefore threatened to withdraw O'Neill and expose his employer's perilous financial status if the money were not paid immediately. Pell had no choice but to give O'Neill the full amount; a short time later the firm went into receivership. Through Commins, O'Neill had escaped just in time. (Other authors, including Theodore Dreiser, Sherwood Anderson, and Robinson Jeffers, were not so fortunate.) In gratitude O'Neill told his next publisher, Random House, that he would join their house only if they would create a position for Commins as editor. O'Neill, in fact, had this stipulation written into his Random House contract. Thus Commins was hired by Bennett Cerf and Donald Klopfer in 1933.[25]

One of the authors with whom he worked was William Faulkner. The Mississippi novelist had begun his period of greatest productivity, and Commins edited the manuscripts of some of his finest novels. *Absalom, Absalom!* was the first book by Faulkner that Commins edited for Random House, and he blue-penciled the setting copy, and later the galleys, quite heavily. Commins questioned the accuracy of Faulkner's statements about southern society, and he argued for the excision of certain material early in the book because the reader would be told about it in more detail later on. Commins attempted to introduce grammatical logic and consistency into the rambling narration of Rosa Coldfield, and he altered the style of the book as well, breaking Faulkner's long sentences into shorter ones, changing words and punctuation, altering rhythms and general syntax. Faulkner was furious, but his previous books, with the single exception of *Sanctuary* in 1931, had been financial failures. Faulkner had no leverage at Random House, and there was little that he could do about Commins's editing. Nevertheless, he tried: he conducted a running battle with the editor in the margins of the typescript and proofs of *Absalom* and succeeded in preserving some of his own characteristic style and word usage.[26]

Faulkner did not have the panache of Gertrude Stein. When Commins questioned the logic of *Four Saints in Three Acts,* she dismissed him with the comment, "My dear, you simply don't understand."[27] And too, Faulkner seems to have liked Commins personally, which may explain why he never asked for another editor at Random House. After he won the Nobel Prize in 1950 Faulkner swung more weight, and the changes in his texts largely ceased. During those final years Commins became a friend and errand runner for Faulkner, much as he had been for O'Neill.

Faulkner was not the only author whose texts changed in Commins's

25. See "The Fall of Liveright," in Dorothy Commins, *What Is an Editor? Saxe Commins at Work* (Chicago: University of Chicago Press, 1978), pp. 12–26; also *"Love and Admiration and Respect": The O'Neill-Commins Correspondence* (Durham, N.C.: Duke University Press, 1986).

26. See James B. Meriwether, *The Literary Career of William Faulkner: A Bibliographical Study* (1961; reprint, Columbia: University of South Carolina Press, 1971), illus. 14; Noel Polk, "The Manuscript of *Absalom, Absalom!" Mississippi Quarterly* 25 (Summer 1972): 359–67; Michael Millgate, *The Achievement of William Faulkner* (New York: Random House, 1966), p. 151.

27. Dorothy Commins, *What Is an Editor?* p. 28.

hands. The editor cut John O'Hara's *A Rage to Live* and altered other O'Hara texts so frequently that the novelist finally rebelled. "You'd better get that surgical glint out of your eye," he wrote in one letter to Commins, and he later became so angry that he is reputed to have thrown a paperweight at the editor's head. O'Hara eventually asked for another editor and was assigned to Albert Erskine.[28]

Perhaps Commins's most unfortunate job of editing involved Robinson Jeffers's final volume of poetry, *The Double Axe*. Jeffers sent the typescript of this book of verse to Random House in 1947, while wartime patriotic feeling was still high. Several of the poems were critical of Franklin D. Roosevelt and Harry Truman. Commins, a Democrat, became angry and insisted that Jeffers cut ten poems from the volume and alter readings in several others. Commins also persuaded Bennett Cerf to print a publisher's disclaimer in the front matter of *The Double Axe*. Jeffers then altered his own preface to respond, rather mildly, to Cerf's remarks. Jeffers had arranged the poems in his manuscript in a sequence designed to demonstrate his philosophy of Inhumanism, and his original prefatory note had explained what he was attempting to do. In the published book, however, the progression of the argument was rendered confusing by the absence of the suppressed poems, and the two prefaces in the opening pages gave conflicting signals to reviewers and readers. According to one Jeffers critic, the book was actually rendered "*more* polemical" and "less aesthetically directed and unified" by Commins's work. Probably without knowing it, Commins had made *The Double Axe* into an "isolated, distempered, sputtering episode" in Jeffers's career. Just why Jeffers did not protest is a mystery. His refusal to fight was consistent with his philosophy of Inhumanism; it is also true that Jeffers was old, ill, and weary by this point and may simply have lacked the energy to protest. Whatever the reason, the published text of *The Double Axe* hindered understanding of Jeffers's thinking and altered the tone and direction of criticism of his poetry for many years after his death.[29]

Commins changed a great many other books significantly. Among the

28. O'Hara to Saxe Commins [Summer 1948], *Selected Letters of John O'Hara*, ed. Matthew J. Bruccoli (New York: Random House, 1978), p. 207. For an account of the paperweight-throwing episode, see Dorothy Commins, *What Is an Editor?* p. 97.

29. James Shebl, *In This Wild Water: The Suppressed Poems of Robinson Jeffers* (Pasadena, Calif.: Ward Ritchie Press, 1976). The quotations are from Robert J. Brophy's foreword. See also Robinson Jeffers, *The Double Axe and Other Poems, Including Eleven Suppressed Poems* (New York: Liveright, 1977).

authors with whom he crossed swords were W. H. Auden and Isak Dinesen. But not all of his authors gave him bad reviews. Irwin Shaw, in his *Paris Review* interview, spoke with gratitude of Commins's attentions to *The Young Lions*. "Editors can be very useful," said Shaw. "I had a great editor, Saxe Commins at Random House, who helped me cut more than a hundred thousand words out of *The Young Lions*. If I had kept them in it might have been a terrible flop." Shaw seems, in fact, to have learned to work comfortably with editors. "The editors I had at the *New Yorker* quietly helped me in peculiar, small ways. One thing they taught me was the value of cutting out the last paragraph of stories, something I pass down as a tip to all writers. The last paragraph in which you tell what the story is about is almost always best left out. The editors I have now are valuable in other ways, occasionally pointing out something they think is a weakness and in getting things straight. In the novel it's hard to keep track of everybody. They also help keep a hold on reality. They say, 'That street didn't run that way.'"[30]

A generally smooth author-editor relationship existed between John Steinbeck and Pascal Covici, who published Steinbeck's fiction first at Covici-Friede and later at Viking Press. Steinbeck came over the years to rely heavily on Covici's judgment. When Covici finished reading *The Grapes of Wrath* in manuscript in January 1939, he wrote to Steinbeck praising the novel but suggesting that the author change the ending of the book.

> Your idea is to end the book on a great symbolic note, that life must go on and will go on with a greater love and sympathy and understanding for our fellowmen. The episode you use in the end is extremely poignant. Nobody could fail to be moved by the incident of Rose of Sharon giving her breast to the starving man yet, taken as the finale of such a book with all its vastness and surge, it struck us on reflection as being all too abrupt. . . . It seems to us that the last few pages need building up. The incident needs leading up to, so that the meeting with the starving man is not so much an accident or chance encounter, but more an integral part of the saga of the Joad family.

Steinbeck disagreed:

> I am sorry but I cannot change that ending. It is casual—there is no fruity climax, it is not more important than any other part of the book—if there is a symbol, it is a survival symbol not a love symbol, it must be an accident, it

30. "Irwin Shaw," in *Writers at Work: The* Paris Review *Interviews,* 5th ser. (New York: Penguin, 1981), p. 164.

must be a stranger, and it must be quick. To build this stranger into the structure of the book would be to warp the whole meaning of the book. The fact
that the Joads don't know him, don't care about him, have no ties to him—
that is the emphasis. The giving of the breast has no more sentiment than the
giving of a piece of bread.

But according to Marshall Best, who was also at Viking in 1939, Steinbeck eventually did alter the last scene. "One of our readers noticed that
Steinbeck had the girl—Rose of Sharon—offering her breast to the
starving man too soon after her baby was born, stillborn and blue. We
pointed this out to Steinbeck and he made a change in that last scene—
he lengthened it to make the act physiologically possible."

The relationship between Steinbeck and Covici eventually became
quite close. Steinbeck's ego was fragile, even after his considerable literary success, and he seems to have needed the attention that Covici provided. To one troubled letter from Steinbeck, full of doubt about his
future as a writer, Covici replied soothingly, "As to yourself, my worry-
ing about you won't help I know. But I, too, see what you can give and I
am jealous for it. In my little life, which is about three-fourths done, you
are my rarest experience. Take that with all its implications, cynically as
well if you want to. The soul of man is not too simple; certainly not for
me. What I do positively know is that I want you to go on."[31]

An editor can be of great assistance to a young author. William Targ, a
bookman, editor, and publisher, describes in his memoirs a session that
he is about to have with a young writer:

> Now to make some notes preparatory to a meeting in my office with a first
> novelist. The manuscript has been read by me; a contract has been signed
> ($4,000 advance) and a bit more work is called for by its author. She is skit-
> tish, reluctant to make further changes or additions—or so it seemed on the
> telephone. I don't want to ruffle her feathers, make a fuss, but . . .
>
> I decide to be persuasive. The first eight pages of her novel introduce nine
> characters, mostly by name. They're faceless. Hard to assimilate. They must be
> established. If one of them were called, say, Popeye, well *that one* would stand
> out. But Allen, Mary, Alexander, Harriet, Lawrence, Fred, et al.—they simply
> must be visible, sketched in somehow.
>
> Chapter three must be cut; it drags. There's too much school minutiae, not
> enough interesting dialogue. Something spiky needed here. The secondary les-
> bian character is shadowy—all we know is that she has a letch for the heroine.

---

31. These various letters are quoted from Thomas Fensch, *Steinbeck and Covici, The Story
of a Friendship* (Middlebury, Vt.: Paul S. Eriksson, 1979), pp. 2, 19; and Peter Lisca, ed., *The
Grapes of Wrath*, Viking Critical Library (New York: Viking, 1972), pp. 857–58.

But what is she *like?* The psychological damage the author is concerned with in the motivating of a strange young boy is not clear at all; calls for something less oblique. Clear the air!

And so on. I make my notes, and at nine-forty-five in comes the author. A lovely young woman. She is surprisingly amenable, amiable, willing to do more work—in full agreement. No contest! She promises to return the manuscript in four days. I promise her lunch if she keeps her word.[32]

Young authors are often very much in need of advice. Hiram Haydn encouraged William Styron to begin a novel in 1948 and secured an advance and a contract from Crown Publishers for the young writer. Throughout the composition of the novel, then titled "Inheritance of Night," Haydn read Styron's drafts and encouraged him to continue. He helped Styron avoid inconsistences in plot and character, and he assisted him in removing echoes of Faulkner and Wolfe from the text. Haydn's changes were small but significant: he showed Styron how to make images of flight and water echo throughout his book and helped him to prune, ever so slightly, some overwritten passages. Haydn moved to Bobbs-Merrill in 1950 and took Styron with him. By then Styron was calling his manuscript *Lie Down in Darkness.* At the last moment, when Styron was struggling to complete the novel, he was recalled into the Marine Corps for the Korean War. Haydn interceded with the draft board and arranged a postponement. The author finished in a last burst, and the novel was published in the fall of 1951. Reviews were almost uniformly laudatory and sales were excellent for a first novel. Examination of the surviving manuscripts and typescripts of the novel confirms that *Lie Down in Darkness* became a better book in Haydn's hands.[33]

A young author is especially grateful for attention and advice from an editor. The relationship can quickly become intimate and intense, and the author can easily develop artistic and emotional ties with the editor. To several long letters, filled with perceptive suggestions from a female editor, one young woman responded this way:

As an editor, you are plain genius and I know two beautiful stars fell and touched each other on the days you and I were born. I also think you wear a

32. *Indecent Pleasures* (New York: Macmillan, 1975), p. 4.

33. Arthur D. Casciato, "His Editor's Hand: Hiram Haydn's Changes in *Lie Down in Darkness,*" *Studies in Bibliography* 33 (1980): 263–73. The surviving fragments of "Inheritance of Night" are at the Duke University Library; the manuscripts and typescripts of *Lie Down in Darkness* are at the Manuscripts Division, Library of Congress, Washington, D.C. See James L. W. West III, "William Styron's *Inheritance of Night:* Predecessor of *Lie Down in Darkness,*" *Delta* (Montpellier), no. 23 (janvier 1986), pp. 1–17.

bandanna and hoop earrings, for forecasting so completely what I have been trying to say in the book. You are also a witch, pick your own spelling, for making me work so damn hard. Worst of all, I think you are a third grade schoolteacher, because when I think I can sneak by with something because I haven't quite understood it myself, you grab me by the seat of my pants and make me go back to my desk and open my answer book. It wouldn't surprise me in the least if you practised face-lifting without a license. I love you.[34]

Years of work in trade houses, however, can eventually cause editors to lose patience with authors, who tend to be emotional and troublesome people even when they are not particularly talented. As Raymond Chandler once put it, writers "have the egotism of actors without either the good looks or the charm."[35] Contempt for authors among editors is not surprising: years of work as a physician can breed a kind of contempt for one's patients, an insensitivity to their pain, just as years of college teaching can encourage indifference toward one's students. Editors must be aware of and guard against this tendency; some are successful in avoiding it, others are not. At its worst, the tendency produces an editor who is arrogant and insensitive and who takes unwarranted liberties with the manuscripts of authors. Editors know what they are expected to say about their role in the creative process, and often they have a standard statement for interviewers and prospective authors. One assumes that most editors do try to keep their professed principles in mind when working with manuscripts. Years of handling troublesome and demanding authors, however, can make an editor callous about their problems and even cynical about the value of the literature they produce. Such an editor thinks that the author cannot know what is best for the book; what the author should do is wait for advice from the editor—and then follow it.

Young authors are particularly vulnerable to high-handed editors because they are eager to be published and will make almost any compromise to see their work in print. An exception, however, was Flannery O'Connor. An early version of the opening of her novella *Wise Blood* had won the Rinehart-Iowa Fiction Award in 1947; Rinehart took an option on the novel and paid O'Connor a $750 advance. The editor to whom she was assigned was John Selby. He read the beginning of her novel, found

34. "Anonymous," in *Editors on Editing,* ed. Gerald Gross (New York: Bowker [1961], 1962), p. 183. Neither the author nor the editor is identified.
35. "Ten Per Cent of Your Life," *Atlantic Monthly* 189 (Feb. 1952): 48.

it unconventional, and sent O'Connor directions for revision. Among his requirements was that she rewrite the novel in first-person narration. O'Connor was offended and responded with this measured reply:

> I can only hope that in the finished novel the direction will be clearer, but I can tell you that I would not like at all to work with you as do other writers on your list. I feel that whatever virtues the novel may have are very much connected with the limitations you mention. I am not writing a conventional novel, and I think that the quality of the novel I write will derive precisely from the peculiarity or aloneness, if you will, of the experience I write from. . . .
>
> In short, I am amenable to criticism but only within the sphere of what I am trying to do; I will not be persuaded to do otherwise. The finished book, though I hope less angular, will be just as odd if not odder than the nine chapters you have now. The question is: is Rinehart interested in publishing this kind of novel? [36]

Selby was not accustomed to prickly statements from young writers, and his relationship with O'Connor quickly deteriorated. The situation was saved by the intervention of Elizabeth McKee, O'Connor's agent, who extricated her from the Rinehart contract and guided her to Robert Giroux at Harcourt, Brace. Giroux worked well with O'Connor. Together with Katherine Anne Porter he made some suggestions for revision but made them in such a way as not to offend the young author. Giroux brought *Wise Blood* into print in 1952, to generally good reviews. By then O'Connor had come to depend on him, and she was uneasy when he left her to join Farrar, Straus. O'Connor apparently thought for a time of following him, but her contract for *Wise Blood* had stipulated that first refusal on her next book should go to Harcourt. She honored the contract but was uneasy until she could meet her new editor, whom she came to like. [37]

Such stories do not always have happy endings. Among the novelists whose work was changed significantly, even damaged, by trade editors are Dashiell Hammett (*Red Harvest*), Edith Summers Kelley (*Weeds*), John Dos Passos (*Three Soldiers*), E. E. Cummings (*The Enormous Room*), Willard Motley (*Knock on Any Door*), James Jones (*From Here to Eternity*), and John Barth (*The Floating Opera*). Kurt Vonnegut and John Updike both had early books altered by editors, but these two au-

---

36. O'Connor to Selby, 18 February 1949, in *The Habit of Being*, ed. Sally Fitzgerald (New York: Farrar, Straus, Giroux, 1979), p. 10.

37. For a sketch of Giroux's career, see Donald Hall, "Robert Giroux: Looking for Masterpieces," *New York Times Book Review*, 6 January 1980, pp. 3ff.

thors, like Barth, have been able to repair the damage in later editions of their work.[38]

Posthumously published manuscripts are also vulnerable to misguided editing. Usually the author has not left specific instructions about publication; often the manuscript is not even in finished form. The author's heirs or literary executors, in collaboration with trade editors, put the drafts into publishable shape. Sometimes the results are successful, sometimes unfortunate. The case of Thomas Wolfe is well known. Edward Aswell carved huge, bleeding chunks from the manuscripts left by Wolfe and, taking editorial liberties that he did not disclose fully, fashioned them into three books. It is a moot point whether the books are legitimately Wolfe's, or whether he would have approved the editing done by Aswell.[39]

All trade editors who work with manuscripts that must be published posthumously face a similar problem: how to make the book salable. The easiest approach is to turn the manuscript into something resembling a novel, because novels are thought to be more marketable than other types of books. Maxwell Perkins was well acquainted with the tendency: "The sales department always want a novel," he wrote Marjorie Kinnan Rawlings in 1933. "They want to turn everything into a novel. They would have turned the New Testament into one, if it had come to us for publication."[40] This kind of thinking had significant consequences for James Agee's posthumously published book *A Death in the Family* (1957). The tirelessly experimental Agee had wanted to publish a volume of autobiographical meditations centering on the death of his own father, something loosely organized and unclassifiable like *Let Us Now Praise Famous Men*. But Agee's heirs and the editors at McDowell, Oblensky turned the manuscript into a novel, even adding to the book one previously published piece of writing by Agee that was not part of the manuscript. It is difficult to argue with their strategy: *A Death in the Family* became a bestseller and won the Pulitzer Prize. It is frequently taught in colleges and

38. Susan Schiefelbein, "Writers, Editors and the Shaping of Books," *Washington Post Book World*, 17 January 1982, pp. 1–2, 8; Randall H. Waldron, "Rabbit Revised," *American Literature* 56 (Mar. 1984): 51–67.

39. John Halberstadt, "The Making of Thomas Wolfe's Posthumous Novels," *Yale Review* 70 (Autumn 1980): 79–94; Leslie Field, *Thomas Wolfe and His Editors: Establishing a True Text for the Posthumous Publications* (Norman: University of Oklahoma Press, 1987).

40. Perkins to Rawlings, 27 October 1933, in *Editor to Author: The Letters of Maxwell E. Perkins*, ed. John Hall Wheelock (New York: Scribners, 1950), p. 84.

universities today. Still, one is uneasy about the book: it is presented to its readers as something it is not, something it was never meant to be.[41]

Editors of posthumously published manuscripts must also satisfy the author's heirs. If the editor is fortunate, these heirs may possess some literary ability and some appreciation for what the author was attempting to do. Dreiser's widow, Helen, however, seems not to have understood fully what he was trying to do in *The Stoic,* and she allowed Dreiser's editor at Doubleday to make cuts and changes that probably should not have been made.[42] Mary Hemingway likewise took it upon herself to cut two chapters from *A Moveable Feast* and an undisclosed amount of material from *Islands in the Stream.*[43] More recently, *The Garden of Eden* has been assembled by a junior editor at Scribners from sections of a much larger Hemingway manuscript. There has been no way of guarding against the attentions of heirs, and many works of literature have been changed significantly as a result.

Trade editors have played central roles in the composition and publication of many important American literary works during this century. Stories of editorial irresponsibility or arrogance are remembered, repeated, and embellished by authors; they are also sought after by literary scholars. Instances of good editing surely outnumber instances of bad editing, but good editing is often forgotten. One of the major problems for scholars who work with twentieth-century American writing—a problem that will demand even more attention in future decades—is to come to terms with the alterations wrought on modern American literature by editors in trade houses. The structure of the typical book-publishing operation in the United States during the first half of the twentieth century put great responsibility on the editor, who often was equal to it but sometimes was not.

Trade editing has not been a static field. Editors who began in the industry during the 1950s have witnessed significant changes in publishing and over the years have altered the way they do business. Samuel S. Vaughan, former president of Doubleday and now senior vice-president and trade editor at Random House, began in the industry in 1952. Initially he held a small editorial job at King Features Syndicate, then

41. Victor A. Kramer, "*A Death in the Family* and Agee's Projected Novel," *Proof* 3 (1973): 139–54.

42. Philip L. Gerber, "Dreiser's *Stoic:* A Study in Literary Frustration," *Literary Monographs* 7 (1975): 85–144.

43. Reynolds, "Words Killed, Wounded, Missing in Action," p. 2.

moved to Doubleday a short while later. He learned publishing from the ground up: he was successively advertising manager and sales manager at Doubleday, became an editor in the late 1950s, and eventually rose to the presidency of the house in 1970. During his tenure as president, he continued much of his work as an editor. Over the course of his career he has handled the work of Bruce Catton, George Garrett, Leon Uris, Irving Stone, Wallace Stegner, and William Buckley. He has also made a specialty of editing the memoirs of important political figures—among them Dwight D. Eisenhower, Hubert Humphrey, and Edmund Muskie. Vaughan is a generalist. He jokes, "As we say, you can have a conversation with an editor like me about anything—for two minutes."[44]

Vaughan has seen many alterations in the industry since 1952. "It seems to me that it was harder to get a book published during the fifties," he said recently. "The act of publishing, the decision to publish, was more of a convulsive act. It no longer requires an amendment to the Constitution to get a book out. Book publishers know that's what they are there for." But the stepped-up pace of decision making has not been entirely a positive thing. "The technology which affects and afflicts us now is not so much the marvelous printing technology; rather, it's the wonderful/awful combination of the photocopy machine and the word processor. In the fifties, things were slower and more deliberate because there simply could not be as many copies of manuscripts made. Today we frequently buy books which are on multiple submissions. If five houses have it, four are wasting their time. Xerography has meant the multiplication of effort for everybody involved. We are buying many things now from outlines or conversations—treatments, in effect, as the movie people say. The failure rate is not going to be improved by such practices."[45]

Robert D. Loomis, vice-president and executive editor at Random House, has much the same perspective on editing as Vaughan. Loomis began in book publishing in 1950 as a reader for Appleton-Century-Crofts, then moved to an editorial job at Rinehart. In 1957 he came to

44. Vaughan has written and lectured widely on the publishing business. See, for example, "The State of the Heart," in *The Business of Book Publishing: Papers by Practitioners,* ed. Elizabeth A. Geiser et al. (Boulder, Colo., and London: Westview Press, 1985); "The Question of Biography," in *Biography and Books,* ed. John Y. Cole (Washington, D.C.: Library of Congress, 1986); and "On Not Looking for a Job," in *Book Publishing Career Directory,* 2d ed. (Hawthorne, N.J.: Career Press, Inc., 1987).

45. These comments and those that follow by Robert D. Loomis are taken from interviews conducted at Random House on 22 September 1987; these remarks are quoted here with permission.

Random House as a senior editor at the invitation of Hiram Haydn. Like Vaughan, Loomis is a generalist, although his lists have been weighted more toward fiction, biography, and history. Among his authors have been William Styron, Jerzy Kosinski, Daniel J. Boorstin, Shelby Foote, Maya Angelou, Woody Allen, and Frederick Exley. He too has worked with political figures—George McGovern, Barry Goldwater, Averell Harriman, and Sam Ervin, Jr.[46]

For Loomis, trade editing has become more complicated and highly pressured since the fifties. "When I first got into this business, the idea of being an editor was pretty much that. You were a good editor, and everything else came from that fact. You did a good job; authors would come to you. You would hold onto the authors you had. In those days, if we got a manuscript in the house that we wanted to publish, we published it. The decision was: Do we want to publish it or don't we? It wasn't: How much can we pay for it, and will Simon and Schuster or Houghton Mifflin pay more? Auctions were almost unheard of. They were so frowned upon, in fact, that the few agents who started them, like Scott Meredith, were almost pilloried."

The manner in which books are purchased and financed has also changed for the editor, who now, as often as not, spends a great amount of time on procurement. Loomis describes the problem: "During the fifties we only paid for the hardcover rights; our advance was predicated on what we would sell in hardcover. If other monies came in, they were beyond what we had judged the advance would be. That made paying advances safer and more predictable. Today, however, we have auctions, and that means you start by paying top dollar for a book and you include all anticipated paperback and book-club revenues. Sometimes you must even get flow-through on your advance from dramatic rights, because you have paid so much. If you are going to pay $400,000 for a book, you'd better make sure that all kinds of money come in against it. Even then it won't work out sometimes, and you won't get the book you want."

For many modern agents, says Loomis, money is almost always the first consideration: "Today—perhaps understandably—a good many agents aren't sending books to the best editors but to the houses that can pay the most. Personally, for the editor, this is very frustrating. It means that no matter how well you do your job, you don't necessarily retain

46. For a sketch of Loomis's career, see "Robert D. Loomis of Random House Wins Fourth Roger Klein Award for Creative Editing," *Publishers Weekly,* 9 May 1977, pp. 25–26.

your authors. Furthermore, if you get most things on multiple submission, you are going to be reading a lot more manuscripts. Everything I get now is via multiple submission. I am given a deadline, two weeks usually, which means I have to read the proposal that week. If I like it, I have to get someone else to look at it because we're going to have to make a bid on it. Then we get into the bidding, and only one house out of five or six can win. This means that a great deal more work is done considering manuscripts which you don't finally buy. Everyone has done the work—they've read the manuscript and want to publish it. And all that work is on top of the actual editing, on top of dealing with the book itself."

Vaughan offers this additional perspective on the purchase of literary properties: "Advances today are advances against *earnings*, not *royalties*. You put up a certain amount of money as an advance on a book; you try to string it out, pay it in installments, but it is guaranteed, really, and it is a guarantee against all earnings. What happened in the sixties and seventies was that originating publishers were asked for more money (or were willing to put up more money) and increasingly we went to paperback people to get some of that money. As a result, the balance of economic power tilted. The paperback publishers became in some cases the primary financers of the operation, the principal bankrollers. Everybody was on a roll, and we sort of rolled down the hill together during the late seventies. That still happens to an extent, but not the way it was happening then."

Both Vaughan and Loomis believe that shopping-center distribution, through such chain outlets as B. Dalton and Waldenbooks, has had a strong effect on publishing. Vaughan remembers when this was not the case: "When I got into the business there was a great tendency to think that the axis of the world was Fifth Avenue—that not a lot happened west of Hoboken. The Saul Steinberg view of the country. When I began, New York and Boston were traditional centers for the booktrade, and Philadelphia was pretty good. One respected certain cities in the Southeast, like Richmond and Atlanta, where there were some enlightened booksellers, mostly in department stores. But Florida wasn't much, and California was a wasteland except for San Francisco. Cleveland was a good book town, oddly enough, and Chicago was a factor because they had good booksellers there, but there were vast stretches of the country which simply weren't part of our working consciousness. This is where mass media and retailing have helped. Given a choice between taking mass retailers and not taking them, I'll take them, because they give us six to ten thousand more places to sell books than we had before."

But mass retail outlets, as both Loomis and Vaughan know, tend to concentrate on the top sellers from the seasonal lists and from the back-list. Blockbuster publishing too has had its effect: "True blockbusters are so big that their initial output in the stores is three or four times what it used to be," says Loomis. "If you get several titles like that in a season, they take up a lot of space in the store. The owner really doesn't have the space to put in all the other books he wants to. His credit is also taxed by those big best-sellers. The midlist and certainly the smaller book is very badly hurt by all of this. It changes something out there." The net effect, according to Loomis, is to change the editor's way of thinking. "Gradually your brain begins to think much more commercially than it used to. It's really fun when it works, of course. Believe me, there are few things greater than handling a best-seller, but it doesn't always happen. Whether it does or doesn't, your brain and your psychological focus are still so much on money that you just don't look at books the way you used to."

Editing will continue to change as book publishing evolves and develops. The editor operates at the point at which author meets publishing house, the juncture at which the work of art begins its transformation into literary merchandise. The editor's power, early and late, has been considerable, and his influence on the eventual published artifact has often been profound.

Chapter 5

The Agent

> I make careers.
>
> —James B. Pinker

Literary agents began to appear in England in the 1840s, and from the beginning they faced strong opposition from publishers. These early agents were a varied group and offered numerous services, including criticism and revision of manuscripts, marketing of manuscripts to publishers or periodicals, and correction of proofsheets. Many early agents were fronts for vanity publishers and pursued authors of high aspiration but small talent. These disreputable types had much to do with establishing a negative attitude among legitimate British publishers toward agents.[1]

Both Sir Walter Scott and Charles Dickens had informal literary agents. As early as the 1820s, Scott was using the two Ballantyne brothers as his agents and, through them, playing the publishers Constable and John Murray against each other. The Ballantynes were printers, and one stipulation of each contract they negotiated was that Scott's novel be manufactured by their firm. Scott was their silent partner and sought thereby to increase his share of the profits without the publisher's knowledge.[2] After 1836, the attorney John Forster functioned as unofficial agent for Dickens. Forster, who was interested in literature and was himself a writer of some ability, seems to have enjoyed the distinction of being Dickens's friend and representative, and he sought no other remuneration. Eventually he would become Dickens's first biographer.[3]

Some of the early authors' societies in England provided the services of literary agencies to their members. This connection is important, for it demonstrates that the rise of the agent grew out of the writer's need for

1. A good account of the advent of the literary agent in England is James Hepburn, *The Author's Empty Purse and the Rise of the Literary Agent* (London: Oxford University Press, 1968). Much of the information in the next several paragraphs is taken from Hepburn's book.

2. J. W. Saunders, *The Profession of English Letters* (London: Routledge and Kegan Paul, 1964), pp. 178–79.

3. Robert L. Patten, *Charles Dickens and His Publishers* (Oxford: Clarendon Press, 1978).

something resembling a trade union—a bargaining tool through which to deal with the publisher. The Guild of Literature and Art (1851), the Association to Protect the Rights of Authors (1875), the Society of Authors (1884), and the Authors' Syndicate (1889) were variously organized to insure authors, to help them through financial difficulties, and to facilitate their dealings with publishers. The only one of these organizations to endure, as we have seen, was the Society of Authors, which still provides some of the services of a literary agency to its members.[4]

The first true literary agents in England, in the sense that we think of agents today, were A. M. Burghes and A. P. Watt. Burghes, who by 1882 was advertising his services in the *Athenaeum,* was of questionable integrity and was eventually taken to court for defrauding several of his clients. Watt, by contrast, was a man of probity and an excellent agent. A self-educated Scot, addicted to books and literature, he began working as an agent around 1875 and was almost immediately successful, probably because he met an existing need among authors. His clients included George Macdonald, Wilkie Collins, Rudyard Kipling, and W. B. Yeats. Usually Watt functioned as a middleman between writers and book publishers, and he flourished partly because he kept the interests of the publishers in mind when he negotiated.

The next important agent to make an appearance in England (in 1896) was James B. Pinker, who during his long career handled work by Joseph Conrad, Arnold Bennett, Stephen Crane, Ford Madox Ford, Oscar Wilde, Henry James, and, for a time, H. G. Wells. Pinker was an odd and sometimes abrasive character; James Joyce and D. H. Lawrence actively disliked him, and he once so enraged Conrad that the author, in a fit of frustration, pushed out the sides of a leather armchair in which he was sitting. But the energetic Pinker was attentive to his clients and was especially useful to them early in their careers. To an "engine for the production of fiction" like Bennett, his services were essential, even after Bennett had attained his fame.[5] To the improvident Conrad he was even

4. See Nigel Cross, *The Common Writer: Life in Nineteenth-Century Grub Street* (Cambridge: Cambridge University Press, 1985), for information about various of the nineteenth-century British societies organized for the protection and charitable support of authors.

5. Pinker's correspondence with Bennett has been published as vol. 1 of *Letters of Arnold Bennett,* ed. James Hepburn (London: Oxford University Press, 1966). The original Pinker-Bennett letters are at the Pattee Library, The Pennsylvania State University, University Park, Pa.

more useful, eventually becoming a personal accountant and close friend of the melancholy author.

The third notable agent to appear in England was Curtis Brown, an American and former newspaperman who had come to England in 1898. From the beginning Brown specialized in foreign copyrights and resales of radio, movie, second serial, translation, and even toy rights. Brown knew the intricacies of international copyright and the Berne Convention; he was responsible for placing the work of several important American authors with British publishers and vice versa. He was a skilled negotiator with whom some publishers did not care to deal. Frederick Macmillan, writing to George Brett, head of the American branch of his publishing house, called Brown "a most objectionable man, who emanates, I am afraid, from your side of the Atlantic."[6]

From the beginning, English literary agents faced strong criticism from established publishers. Their most vocal opponent was William Heinemann, who called them "parasites." Heinemann's attacks resulted in part from his belief that agents destroyed the possibility of friendly relations between publishers and authors, but his opposition stemmed originally from a more direct cause: early in his career he had lost the chance to publish Rudyard Kipling's works because of the intervention of an agent.

The legitimacy of agents, their ethics and their real usefulness to the author, were matters of frequent printed debate in England from the mid-1880s to 1900. Opponents of the literary agent were vocal and insistent, but in the end they had no real effect. The agent proved to be useful to the author, and publishers began to recognize that agents could be helpful to them as well by taking over many of the small and unprofitable aspects of publishing, such as handling anthology reprint rights or arranging for lecture appearances. By the turn of the century, agents had become a permanent feature of the British literary scene.

Perhaps their most important contribution to the author's lot had to

6. Macmillan to Brett, 4 March 1908, James Lane Allen file, Macmillan Papers, Manuscripts Division, New York Public Library. Brown's opinion of Macmillan was apparently not a great deal more favorable. In a letter to Sir Frederick of 16 June 1915, he politely accuses the publisher of trying to do him out of his share of movie-right money to Thomas Hardy's *Far from the Madding Crowd*. The letter is in the Macmillan Archives at the British Library, London, BL Add. MS 54888. Brown published his reminiscences under the title *Contacts* (London: Cassell, 1935).

do with how authors were paid. Before the advent of agents, it was customary for authors either to sell publishers the copyrights to their works for flat fees or to take payments on the half-profits arrangement. The former system had its advantages: the author received the money in a lump sum before publication, and the publisher assumed the entire risk of the venture. If the work became unusually popular and outsold the publisher's preliminary estimate, however, the author did not share in the extra proceeds. The half-profits system in theory allowed the author to share the risk of publication and to receive 50 percent of the income, once expenses of manufacture had been recovered. The system, however, encouraged abuses; publishers were sometimes guilty of working in hidden surcharges on production and distribution or of concealing discounts to booksellers so that they actually took their profits two times. Some of them then refused to open their records to authors and, by law, could not be compelled to do so. Mark Twain published *The Innocents Abroad* in England on half-profits, and William Dean Howells published several editions in England under the same arrangement, but neither man was satisfied. British authors were also unhappy with the system, and through their agents and the Society of Authors they began to insist on royalty arrangements.[7] Under such contracts the author also shared the risk of publication but stood to profit in proportion to the commercial success of the book. An author could give the publisher an added incentive to market the book vigorously by extracting a cash advance through an agent. Publishers naturally did not favor these arrangements at first, but by 1900 royalty contracts were becoming standard. British agents also succeeded after 1891 in substantially reducing the share of American rights reserved by the British publisher.

This was an important concession because the American market had become profitable to the British author in a small way, even before the international copyright legislation of 1891. Since the late 1820s English writers and publishers had been receiving flat payments from established American houses for advance proofsheets, from which American editions could be typeset. The arrangement gave the American publisher only a few days' jump over less ethical pirates, but it paid for itself in increased

7. For an explanation of the advantages and disadvantages of the profit-sharing arrangement, see Stanley Unwin, *The Truth about Publishing*, rev. ed. (London: Allen and Unwin, 1946), pp. 64ff.

goodwill with the British, and it helped prepare the way for the trans-atlantic copyright law.[8]

Informal literary agents were operating in America as early as the 1820s. James Lawson, a Scot by birth, came to New York City in 1815, where he worked as an accountant for his uncle. He devoted substantial amounts of time to literary matters and became unofficial agent for William Cullen Bryant, James Kirke Paulding, Edgar Allan Poe, William Gilmore Simms, John Greenleaf Whittier, and others. He was also friendly with the actor Edwin Forrest; through Lawson many plays were submitted to Forrest for consideration. Lawson built up a network of friendships by doing favors and making small loans to publishers and editors. His negotiating powers were strengthened by these connections and by the fact that he charged his authors no fee. He sought to be gentlemanly in all dealings, an approach that made him the more effective. The appearance of leisure and detachment has always been one of the qualities an agent must cultivate. The publisher would much rather deal with a relaxed, objective agent than with a debt-pressed, importunate author.[9]

By 1827, the U.S. Consul to London, Thomas Aspinwall, had begun to function as literary agent for Washington Irving in England. Aspinwall represented Irving successfully in dealings with the publisher John Murray; later he negotiated with other publishers on behalf of James Fenimore Cooper, Jared Sparks, and William Hickling Prescott. Aspinwall, unlike Lawson, took a percentage of the author's receipts in return for his services. Initially he charged a commission of only 2.5 percent, but by 1840 he was receiving 10 percent. Aspinwall sometimes acted as banker for his authors. English publishers often gave promissory notes or bills of exchange to authors instead of cash payments; Aspinwall held these notes and used them as collateral to borrow money for his clients. Sometimes he even advanced money to authors out of his own pocket. Aspinwall

8. Rights to publish a book in America were established by announcing the intention to do so. Such announcements were printed in newspapers or trade circulars. Precedence was sometimes an issue of dispute, especially with Harper and Brothers, who did not always respect the prior claims of other publishers to potentially salable titles. In the Harper Archive at the Pierpont Morgan Library, New York, for example, is a letter from D. Appleton and Company to Harper and Brothers, dated 21 April 1831, in which Appleton insists that they advertised an upcoming edition of "Clara, or Slave Life" on 18 March, three days before Harpers announced its own intention to publish the book.

9. Thomas L. McHaney, "An Early 19th Century Literary Agent: James Lawson of New York," *Papers of the Bibliographical Society of America* 64 (2d Qtr., 1970): 177–92.

frequently helped arrange for simultaneous publication of works in England and America. He was familiar with the intricate British copyright laws and could orchestrate simultaneous releases in such a way as to protect his authors' rights on both sides of the Atlantic.[10]

By the 1840s Park Benjamin was working as a literary agent in New York. Benjamin is most frequently remembered today as one of the editors of the cheap weekly *Brother Jonathan,* a newspaper that pirated the work of established British novelists and caused great difficulties for more dignified but no less piratical American publishers. Benjamin lost his inheritance in the Panic of 1837 and thereafter turned to newspaper work, journalism, and occasional publishing for his livelihood. He operated an informal literary agency during the 1840s and handled some of Henry Wadsworth Longfellow's work of that period. Benjamin also ran a lecture bureau for authors. Initially he charged no fee or commission for these services; his rewards were the goodwill of authors, editors, and publishers. By the early 1860s, however, he had begun to ask for remuneration. His 1863 advertising flyer promised that for a fee of ten dollars he would "assist authors" by reading their manuscripts critically and giving a "candid opinion." If he approved the manuscript, he would recommend it to a publisher. "Letters of inquiry or asking advice," he added, "should always cover a small fee, to compensate time and trouble in replies."[11]

In the 1870s and 1880s there were several literary agencies in New York, including the Athenaeum Bureau of Literature, the New York Bureau of Literary Revision, and the Writer's Literary Bureau. American authors' societies, like their English counterparts, performed some of the services of literary agencies. The Association of American Authors, for example, published a journal, provided information on the costs of publication, arbitrated disagreements between authors and publishers, and supplied funds to needy members. All of these early agents, paid and unpaid, offered writers the advantage of having a representative in New York, which by then was already becoming the publishing center of the country. The author could live and write elsewhere but enjoy the advantage of face-to-face bargaining through an agent.

10. James J. Barnes and Patience P. Barnes, "Thomas Aspinwall: First Transatlantic Literary Agent," *Papers of the Bibliographical Society of America* 78 (3d Qtr., 1984): 321–31.
11. Lillian B. Gilkes, "Park Benjamin: Literary Agent, *et cetera,*" *Proof* 1 (1971): 35–89. Benjamin's advertising flyer is reproduced on p. 87.

The first successful and influential literary agent in America was Paul Revere Reynolds. He was born in Boston in 1864; his father and paternal grandfather were prosperous physicians, and the family had impeccable New England roots. Reynolds attended Boston Latin School and the Adams Academy in Quincy, then entered Harvard, where he was a classmate of George Pierce Baker and a student of William James. Reynolds took his baccalaureate degree in 1887 and worked briefly for the Boston publishing house D. Lothrop and Company before returning to Harvard in 1888 to study for an M.A. under James. Reynolds was much influenced by James, who once said that the young Bostonian had the most honest mind of any student he had ever taught. The years under James's tutelage were perhaps the most satisfying and stimulating in Reynolds's life (one of his fellow students was George Santayana), and he took his master's degree with honors in 1891.

Reynolds wanted to be a writer but did not have the talent; at the age of twenty-seven he was becoming a burden on his family. He had worked briefly during the summer of 1889 as a manuscript reader for *Youth's Companion,* and this experience seems to have suggested to him that he might make his living as a reader or editor in New York. He went there in 1891 and almost by accident became the American agent for the books of the English publisher Cassell. His duties were to place Cassell's books with American publishers and to dispose of plates or printed sheets from a list supplied by the London office. He also served as a scout for Cassell and attempted to secure English rights to promising books or to magazine material for his employer. For his services he was paid five hundred dollars annually. Reynolds was an energetic worker. He met many of the prominent American writers, editors, and publishers of the day, and by 1893 he had become the American representative for William Heinemann and for Sampson Low. He had also begun to work on commission for individual authors, handling their book and magazine submissions from his office at 70 Fifth Avenue.

Reynolds's main activity during these years was to function as intermediary between British and American publishing interests. International copyright had come in 1891, and with it had come many new opportunities for writers and publishers on both sides of the Atlantic. Reynolds did much of his work for British houses like Constable, and he frequently cooperated with the London agents Curtis Brown and James Pinker. The American international copyright act had brought many new problems. It was essentially a protectionist measure and did not provide for free passage of printed materials back and forth between the United States and Great Britain. The printers' unions in America had had a strong voice in the framing of the Chace Act—as this measure was called—and they had succeeded in incorporating into it a manufacturing restriction aimed directly at the British printing industry. In order for a work of literature to enjoy the protection of copyright under the Chace Act, it had to be typeset, printed, and bound in the United States. This made it impossible for American publishers to function simply as large-scale distributors for stock sent over by British houses. There was, by contrast, no such restriction in Great Britain, and publishers there could take plates, sheets, or bound stock from American houses for British distribution, with full protection of their own domestic copyright.

The Chace Act was an irritation to British publishers but a blessing for literary agents on both sides. Transatlantic piracy was no longer much of a threat—on new books, at any rate—but the complexities of joint British-American publication had increased. Authors and even publishers were not always sure who owned what percentages of what rights. Authors frequently compounded the difficulties by agreeing to sell rights that they did not in fact possess. Agents like Reynolds, experienced in such matters, were called upon to untangle the problems.

Reynolds handled U.S. rights for Wells, Wilde, Conrad, and George Meredith; his American authors included Robert W. Chambers, Joel Chandler Harris, Frank Norris, and Stephen Crane. Reynolds was especially useful to Crane, who was careless about business matters and irresponsible with money. Reynolds extricated Crane from a contract he had unwisely signed with the S. S. McClure Syndicate, and he functioned as Crane's unofficial banker, making advance payments to him on unsold stories. This was not standard practice, but an agent was usually willing to advance money against work in progress when an author's work was in great demand—as Crane's was.

Reynolds was known as a "double agent." That is, he worked for both authors and publishers. Like A. P. Watt, he understood that it was important to stay on good terms with publishers because agents had to address them repeatedly on behalf of many different authors. The wise agent did not attempt to drive an unfair bargain on the author's behalf. An imbalanced contract or an overly large advance would put the publisher at an initial disadvantage and take away the funds and incentive needed to advertise and distribute the book successfully.[12]

The first American agents were not accepted immediately by New York publishers. These publishers had always enjoyed an advantage in face-to-face dealings with authors, and they did not wish to lose their edge. They disliked being forced to bid against one another for an author's work and argued that the author should accept less advantageous terms in order to keep all work "under one roof," where it could be promoted in such a way that each book would help sell its fellows. Publishers also resented the implication that they were sharp or dishonest dealers. They maintained that the publisher's interests were identical to the author's: both wanted to produce a good book that would sell to as many readers as possible. These publishers neglected to mention, or failed to realize, that all author-publisher dealings are initially of an adversary nature. Within reason, publishers wish to secure the right to manufacture and sell literary work on terms most advantageous to their houses. Authors wish to receive the highest payment possible for their labors and to retain as many of the subsidiary rights, or percentages of them, as they can. By the early years of this century, publishing had become so complicated and so potentially profitable that an agent had to be mindful of the author's interests, not of the publisher's.

Only a few decades before, American authors had dealt directly with printer-publishers in all details of manufacture and sales. The results usually had been unsatisfactory from a financial standpoint, but writers had been able to exert immediate influence over production and marketing of their work—the look of the physical volume and the manner in which it was sold. When publishers began to function separately and to job out the manufacturing of books, however, they became middlemen; and by the late 1880s heads of publishing houses had begun to employ editors and other subordinates to insulate themselves from authors. Authors lost control over their work once it had been placed in the hands of publishers. Faced with this situation, authors had no choice but to employ literary agents.

The great contribution of the literary agent was to see that publication of an author's book was not a monolithic operation. Book publishing

12. Frederick Lewis Allen, *Paul Revere Reynolds* (New York: privately published, 1944).

was (and is) in reality a sequence of numerous small tasks, some routine and not very important but others—such as the design of the binding and jacket or the organization and financing of the sales campaign—crucial to the success of the book and to the creation of a recognizable public image for the author. Agents learned not to assign control of all these various tasks to the publisher automatically. Some of the chores, such as disposition of certain subsidiary rights, they reserved for themselves; others, such as the writing of jacket copy and advertising material, they assigned to the publisher only conditionally, subject to final approval by both agent and author before release.

Reynolds and his fellow agents sometimes had difficulty with American publishers. Henry Holt proved especially quarrelsome and seemed actually to enjoy sparring with agents in his correspondence. (It must also be said that Reynolds, in office memos and private communications, displayed a certain relish for making magazine editors and book publishers come to heel.) Not surprisingly, the surviving Holt-Reynolds correspondence, preserved among the Holt archives at Princeton, is unfriendly in tone. In the earliest surviving letters, dated 1897, Reynolds is representing such English publishers as Constable, Heinemann, Hutchinson, and Unwin. The correspondence concerns matters of international copyright and the shipping of printed sheets or electrotype plates back and forth across the Atlantic. In his letters to Holt, Reynolds presses for decisions about particular books; Holt, in his communications, complains about damage to plates during shipment or about the fact that English electros will not fit on American presses. By 1903 the correspondence has become snippy: Holt balks at an English publisher's insistence (communicated through Reynolds) that an American book be typeset with British spelling, else the publisher will not order sheets from Holt. And Reynolds tells Holt, in a letter fully two pages long, to stop making pencil marks on manuscripts if he does not intend to purchase them for publication.

By early 1906 the two men were tangling in earnest through the mails. During a bidding war over rights to a potential best-seller from England, Reynolds was moved to state his own principles: "The agent may stimulate such conditions [bidding for books by rival publishers] and undoubtedly in some cases he has done so," he wrote to Holt, "but he does not create them. You do not seem to me to allow in your scheme for legitimate competition." Holt was not persuaded:

You say I don't seem to you to allow for legitimate competition. In publishing, I don't think a competition *merely* of dollars and cents is legitimate. Steady relations, when good ones, are better for the author than jumping around to catch pennies, even many pennies; and when the jumping around leads . . . to realizing by an immediate grab, only half as many pennies during a few months as would have been realized by depending on legitimate returns, the policy seems doubly bad.[13]

Holt never became entirely reconciled to the presence of the literary agent in American publishing, nor did Charles Scribner, who as late as 1913 was advising George Washington Cable not to let Reynolds handle serial rights to one of his novels. "It would not be advisable to have it hawked about by his organization in the thoughtless way such things are sometimes done," wrote Scribner to Cable.[14] Less traditional American publishers, however, were not so hostile to agents. George H. Doran, Frank Doubleday, S. S. McClure, and Horace Liveright recognized that agents could be valuable buffers between authors and publishing houses and that agents could often put publishers in touch with the kinds of material they wanted to issue. It is typical of the American way of doing things that publishers in the United States, unlike their English counterparts, did not spend much time debating the legitimacy or efficacy of the literary agent. Once agents had become established in the literary market-

13. The Holt-Reynolds correspondence is in Box 104 of the Henry Holt Papers, Manuscripts Division, Princeton University Library, Princeton, N.J. The letters quoted or summarized here are Reynolds to Holt, 1 March 1897, 27 July 1900, 5 June 1903, and 30 January 1906; Holt to Reynolds, 13 February 1906; Holt to Pinker, 2 February and 1 March 1904; Pinker to Holt, 15 and 16 February 1904. There is another interesting exchange in the Holt Papers, this one between Henry Holt and S. S. McClure. To Holt, McClure represented much that he disapproved of in the "new" approach to publishing. On 25 September 1915, Holt wrote McClure, "When I entered the publishing business, self-respecting publishers did not go for each other's authors: it was a case of honor among thieves; for there was no international copyright law; and we all helpt ourselves to foreign authors, but not intentionally to each other's authors. The business was then really high-toneder (to quote good John Hay) than it has been since." McClure, who had poached one or two authors from Holt in the past, answered two days later: "You know, looking back over history we find that publishing firms grow old and decay and younger and more successful firms come along, and it would hardly be right that authors should stay with the decaying institution in place of taking up with a more virile, younger institution, so I think that human nature will probably control these matters." Holt responded on 2 October, "I have been a good deal of an idealist in this matter—too much perhaps, as in some others. I have thought that the relation between publisher and author should be like that between lawyer and client and physician and patient, and that publishers should not interfere with each other any more than men in those other professions do."
14. Scribner to Cable, 19 September 1913, Box 28, Scribner Archive, Princeton University Library, Princeton, N.J.

place, most American publishers adapted and began to look for ways to shift some of the troublesome and unprofitable aspects of the publishing business—fielding reprint requests or handling offers for nickel-and-dime foreign rights, for example—onto the shoulders of agents. Some publishers even came to prefer dealing with agents rather than with authors. As Benjamin Huebsch put it, "You may be a talented author and a lucrative author, but you may be a damned nuisance personally. In that case, the publisher would rather have you represented by an agent who is not a damned fool."[15] Doran, who felt similarly, explained his position in some detail in his memoirs:

> I have had large dealings with literary agents, and if I had my publishing life to live over again I would choose, except in isolated instances, to deal with authors through a reputable agent rather than with the authors direct. In the first instance, it protects the publisher from charges of unfairness. An agent, through his knowledge of general publishing conditions and practice, is often able to explain satisfactorily some point in question. Again, it is a convenience to a publisher to be able to confer with literary agents and ascertain quickly what books and authors are open for negotiation. On the whole, I feel that the literary agent has been a constructive force in modern publishing.[16]

Like most American industries, publishing was dominated by men during the first half of the twentieth century. One of the earliest and best ways for a woman to enter publishing was to work as a literary agent. Women faced less discrimination in this field than in any other branch of publishing, and they quickly proved themselves adept and successful. The first female agent in America was Flora May Holly, who came from an established family in Stamford, Connecticut. She attended private schools in her native state and business school in New York, then went to work at the *Bookman* in the mid-1890s. "I was receptionist before that word was used, secretary, contributor and all round editorial assistant at the sum of $20 a week," she later recalled. In the late 1890s she rented an office at 156 Fifth Avenue and began her own literary agency. At work she was businesslike, but on Friday evenings she transformed her apartment into a salon for the literati of the city. At various times in her career, Holly represented Theodore Dreiser, Gertrude Atherton, Agnes Sligh Turnbull, Edna Ferber, and Noel Coward. Most of the writers she handled,

15. Benjamin Huebsch, Oral Memoir, Columbia University Oral History Collections, Butler Library, New York, p. 80.
16. George H. Doran, *Chronicles of Barabbas, 1884–1934* (London: Methuen, 1935), p. 93.

however, specialized in light fiction—romances and detective novels. Early in her career, an editor at *McCall's* told her that most popular stories involved overcoming obstacles and achieving goals, and she frequently passed that advice along to her authors. She learned to coach them on the composition of what she called "the lending library sort of book." Like most early agents, she took what business came her way. One prospective client, for example, wrote her that he was currently making his living by "lecturing with 100 kodachrome slides which I took in Rarotonga" and accompanying himself on the accordion and guitar.[17]

Literary agents were not above pursuing successful authors. Paul Revere Reynolds began to court Booth Tarkington late in 1911, and by October 1912 Tarkington had agreed to let Reynolds handle his fiction and articles on a trial basis for one year. Reynolds was immediately tested: S. S. McClure had been negotiating with Tarkington for a series of four stories at $1,200 each and did not want to close the deal through an agent. In an attempt to circumvent Reynolds, McClure dispatched his son-in-law, Cameron Mackenzie, to visit Tarkington in Indiana. Word of this impending visit leaked to Reynolds, who quickly wrote to Tarkington urging that Mackenzie be referred to him in New York. Reynolds promised to get a higher price from McClure, and Tarkington was persuaded. (The matter was resolved equivocally. Tarkington had no series in mind at the time, so Reynolds got McClure to settle for a single story, but at a price of $1,750.)

Tarkington had built up cordial relationships with several magazine editors, and he apparently feared that Reynolds would disrupt his dealings with them. In his agreement with the agent, he therefore stipulated that he would continue personally to market his stories to the *Saturday Evening Post, Collier's,* and the *Century.* Reynolds agreed but was not happy about the arrangement, inasmuch as the *Post* and *Collier's* were two of the highest-paying slicks in New York. Tarkington also wanted to retain the right to place serial versions of his novels with magazines. Again Reynolds agreed but kept prodding Tarkington in succeeding months, using inside information and the enticement of more money:

17. The Holly Papers are in the Manuscripts Division, New York Public Library. Quotations and information are taken from an untitled autobiographical document (ca. 1932); from notes for "The Town Clerk's Daughter"; from Holly to Cora A. Jenks, 19 December 1942; and from Loring Andrews to Holly, 30 July 1942. Holly seems to have spelled her middle name both "May" and "Mai."

I want to say if you have a new serial coming along, I do not see why it wouldn't be business for you to say to me, "I sold my last serial for so much money. If you can get me more, and enough more to make it worth while, I will pay you a commission. Otherwise not".

I think "The Flirt" [Tarkington's most recent serial] could have been sold for more money than you got for it, from what I learn, and if there is more money floating around here I think it is a mistake for us to let it float. Don't you?

But Tarkington kept handling his own serial rights. He also continued to deal personally with a few magazines and thereby created a problem for Reynolds: other magazine editors complained that favored competitors were getting Tarkington's work at cheaper rates than those Reynolds was making them pay. Reynolds continued to pursue Tarkington, asking for a "definite agreement" but not a binding one. "I wouldn't hold any author against his will," wrote Reynolds, "no matter whether I had a cast iron contract or not, and least of all you." Tarkington was never entirely persuaded, however, and until the end of his career he handled some of his own negotiations with editors.[18]

Early in their careers many authors do not realize the usefulness of a literary agent. To young authors, the agent is simply one more person making money from their writing. Referring to his agents at Curtis Brown, W. H. Auden wrote to Bennett Cerf in October 1936: "What goes on in that office and what they do for the 10% of my hard earned money I cannot imagine." In a later communication Auden was even more blunt. There had been a misunderstanding about a £50 advance, and Auden needed the money. "Curtis Brown is an inefficient ninny," he fumed, and Cerf agreed. "I wish to heaven we could deal with each other direct!" he wrote Auden. To Curtis Brown, Cerf fired off this telegram: "ARE YOU AUDENS AGENTS OR ARE YOU NOT?"[19]

But a few years later Auden began to realize how useful his literary agents had become to him. Auden collaborated in a variety of forms—prose, verse, drama, and opera—and it fell to his agents to determine what percentages of which rights went to whom and on what time schedule payments should be made. Particularly troublesome, for ex-

18. The Reynolds-Tarkington correspondence is in the P. R. Reynolds Papers, Butler Library, Columbia University, New York. Quotations and information are taken from Reynolds to Tarkington, 14 and 21 October 1912, 14 February 1913, and 24 January 1914; Tarkington to Reynolds, 16 October 1912 and 4 March 1914.

19. Random House Papers, Columbia University, New York. Quotations from Auden to Cerf, 6 October and undated [mid-October 1936]; Cerf to Auden, 14 October 1936; Cerf to Curtis Brown, undated telegram.

ample, were the tangled negotiations over Auden's work with Bertolt Brecht on a production of *The Duchess of Malfi*. So extensive were the disagreements that Curtis Brown eventually had to take the case to the Dramatists Guild for arbitration. Once Auden's reputation was established, frequent requests to reprint his poems, one or two or three at a time, in anthologies and textbooks and even on Hallmark Christmas cards, came into the Curtis Brown offices. At least one such request arrived nearly every week. Handling this correspondence took much time and yielded small change; Auden came to realize that it was a great advantage to have his agents attend to these matters for him.

Still, Auden was not a model author from an agent's standpoint. He seems not to have been aware of the many ways in which his work could be made to yield income. He would occasionally allow composers to set his verse to music, gratis, apparently not realizing that his agents could collect for such adaptations through ASCAP, the American Society of Composers, Authors, and Publishers. Auden also had a tendency to deal directly with magazine editors and, as a result, to take a lower fee than his agents would have accepted. ("May I suggest that you only do yourself in the eye by sending off pieces direct to editors?" wrote Alan C. Collins of Curtis Brown to Auden.) Eventually Auden's agents broke him of these habits, and by the 1960s he was routinely referring all literary business to them. By this time the volume had become immense—partly because Auden was prolific and partly because his work was very popular. Auden could never have handled all the requests and business propositions himself.[20]

Not all of the poetry handled by the Curtis Brown agency was so elevated artistically as Auden's. One of their most active accounts was with Ogden Nash, who not only wrote verse but also penned lyrics to musical comedies. Nash found it useful to negotiate through an agent. In the middle of an extended wrangle about the various subsidiary rights to a show headed for Broadway (or so he hoped), Nash almost lost his equanimity. "Why is it that everybody west of Sixth Avenue is temperamental?" he lamented. Fortunately, his agents could deal with the various personalities, leaving Nash free to compose. He covered his expenses during such slack periods by going on the lecture circuit. Detailed arrangements were always made by his agent, but the trips were still ener-

20. Auden files, Curtis Brown Collection, Columbia University, New York. The quotation is from Collins to Auden, 8 August 1957.

vating. On a Pullman heading west to Chicago, Nash had plenty of time to contemplate the upcoming schedule and to write a letter to Collins at Curtis Brown. Nash's first lecture date, he reminded Collins, was in Minneapolis; then he would head south to Texas. "Lubbock," he mused, "lubly Lubbock," and signed the letter with "Lub—." During the long train ride, Nash entertained himself by penning irreverent answers to a questionnaire he discovered in a copy of *Ladies' Home Journal* that a fellow traveler had left on the seat. The title of the questionnaire was "Why Can't a Woman Be More Like a Man?" Because he thought it might amuse her, Nash sent the completed questionnaire to Edith Haggard, another of the agents at Curtis Brown. She promptly had it typed up and mailed to an editor at *Ladies' Home Journal* who paid $350 for publication rights. Nash's doodling had paid off, with an agent's help.

Nash wrote much of his light verse to order. Magazine editors and greeting-card manufacturers supplied ideas to him through his agents, and he knocked out the limericks and rhymes. Last-minute details such as an alteration of "tarts" to "tramps" in one poem and the repair of an imperfect Italian rhyme in another fell to his agents, and they fielded the surprisingly frequent requests to reprint Nash's poems for no payment. To judge from the correspondence, many people seem to have assumed that because Nash's verse was humorous, he must have written it just for fun.[21]

Agents became more useful as the possible ways for an author to republish or adapt earlier work increased in number, but the agent had to be energetic, persistent, and imaginative in attempting to exploit the earning potential of a given literary property. Most of all an agent needed experience and a wide circle of contacts. Agents, like publishers and editors, went through no training program and passed no certification exam. Anyone could become an agent, simply by claiming the title. The temptation was great to make the easy and expected sales, collect the 10 percent commission, and leave the difficult work alone. For this reason authors had to be careful in choosing their agents.

Most agents insisted on handling each client's entire literary output. In turn, the agent received 10 percent of the literary income of the writer, even when the writer occasionally handled a sale alone. Many authors

21. Nash files, Curtis Brown Collection. Quotations from Nash to Alan C. Collins, 27 May 1949; Nash to Edith Haggard, undated.

balked at this condition, and agents accordingly began to require written contracts to stipulate the conditions of the relationship. Occasionally an agent would make an exception for a big-name author because being known as that author's agent provided prestige and helped bring in other business. F. Scott Fitzgerald, for example, dealt directly with Scribners on all of his books but routed his magazine work through his agent, Harold Ober.

The agent undoubtedly was correct in claiming 10 percent of the writer's entire literary earnings. Pinker stated the argument forcefully in a letter to Arnold Bennett, who had protested the payment to Pinker of 10 percent on some journalism that Bennett had himself marketed. Pinker responded:

> The amount involved is so small that one is tempted not to argue about it. I should therefore leave it to you to decide as you please but for the principle involved, which is, of course, what interests you too. You would, I know, be the first to admit that you were able to sell those articles on those terms because of my work in building up your market. If when the market is worked up an author is going to take pieces of business into his own hands he will naturally take all the easy pieces and leave the agent the difficult ones. That would be most unfair to the agent, and it would end in changing the whole relationship. As you know, it frequently happens that there is work to do for an author which involves no commission for the agent, or a commission so insignificant as to be negligible, but at the same time it is work that the author particularly wishes done. One does it with the good will and energy that one applies to the more profitable business, but only because one has towards the author the feeling of complete service. If the author is to take isolated items of his business and withhold commission, the agent is bound to react and withhold his services where they would yield no immediate commission.[22]

Contractual arrangements were to the advantage of the agent because they ensured that the labor an agent had invested on the sale of a given literary property would yield dividends for many years, even if the author left the agent. Many authors did not understand this condition fully, but they quickly learned its implications when they switched to other literary agents. Though the author was not actively associated with the first agent, that agent continued to handle the properties that the author had produced while a client of the agency. Such an arrangement discouraged authors from leaving one agent for another; among other considerations,

22. Quoted in Hepburn, *The Author's Empty Purse*, pp. 62–63.

the author knew that the first agent, if so minded, could take a kind of perverse revenge by giving less than full attention to old but still valuable literary properties.

Some authors chafed under these obligations, among them novelist Raymond Chandler, who unburdened himself in an article entitled "Ten Per Cent of Your Life," published in the *Atlantic Monthly:*

> Among all those quasi-professional businesses which like to refer to their customers as clients the business of literary agenting is probably the most enduring and the most adhesive. Technically, you can fire your agent; it is a sticky operation, but a determined man can achieve it. It really ends nothing. Years after you speak to him you will, if you are a writer for publication, be finding mud tracks across the carpet. He will have been there in the night doing what he calls "representing" you, and you will wake up in the morning with that tired feeling as if a Doberman pinscher had been sleeping on your chest. It was probably only a little old foreign book royalty that he nibbled at, a trivial matter in dollars and cents. But the nibbling goes on forever. Long after your agent has been gathered to his fathers, you may be paying commissions to his estate on some transaction with which he had hardly any contact, something purely automatic that arose out of something else long before.

Chandler was writing here of legitimate agents who were looking after their own interests—something Chandler and other authors could at least understand. Chandler reserved a particular contempt, however, for a variant species of literary agent who preyed on the young and untalented—"racketeers of hope," he called them, "whose real income is from reading fees and from such charges as they can impose on their 'clients' for editing and revising work which any reputable commission man would know in the beginning to be hopeless." Chandler's suspicion about the literary agent was the common distrust of any creative artist for the broker. "His function is too vague," wrote Chandler, "his presence always seems one too many, his profit looks too easy, and even when you admit that he has a necessary function, you feel that this function is, as it were, a personification of something that in an ethical society would not need to exist. If people could deal with one another honestly, they would not need agents." [23]

Most authors welcomed attention and help from their agents, however, and by the early 1900s agents were advising authors on career direction, on which genres to develop, and on what material to exploit.

23. "Ten Per Cent of Your Life," *Atlantic Monthly* 189 (Feb. 1952): 48, 50.

Agents also began to read, critique, and revise manuscripts. In giving advice and working on manuscripts, agents naturally could be counted on to keep commercial possibilities in mind because their livelihoods depended on their success in marketing literary work. The agent encouraged in the serious author a healthy attitude toward the business of writing, an acceptance of the idea that literary work could be artistically challenging and, at the same time, financially remunerative. The agent became a means by which commercial considerations and popular taste exerted influence on the author's work, a way in which the tension between art and commerce was communicated to the author.

Many agents began to function as editors, offering criticism and suggesting cuts and revisions, often refusing to offer a manuscript to a publisher or a periodical until it had been revised, rewritten, and polished. The agent's role here was crucial. A good agent wanted every manuscript to sell to the first buyer to whom it was sent. This was an unrealistic goal, of course, but the agent aimed for it nevertheless. The author would receive payment more quickly; the agent would collect a commission almost immediately. Too, the agent would not waste time for which, in effect, there would be no pay. Toward this end, the agent wanted publishers and magazines to receive clean, crisp typescripts, with no lifeless characters, confused time schemes, or blurry plots.

An example from F. Scott Fitzgerald's career helps make the point. During the summer of 1933, Fitzgerald needed money urgently to meet his wife's hospitalization expenses and to pay his overdue income tax bill. He therefore persuaded his agent, Harold Ober, to submit some less than fully finished writing to the *Saturday Evening Post* and to press the editors there for a decision. The *Post* editors saw that the stories had been hurriedly composed and turned them down. Ober recognized the problem and, in his next letter to Fitzgerald, outlined a sensible strategy for submitting future work:

> Before we show the next story to the Post I think we ought to be sure that it is just right, I think I ought to have it properly typed, and I want to try to create the impression that I am sending them a Scott Fitzgerald story, that it is a fine story and that I don't care whether they take it or not. I am sure it is a mistake for the Post to feel that you are uncertain about a story and anxious to know whether or not they like it.
>
> I would like to start to create this new impression with this new story you are writing. I think perhaps by trying to gain a day or two we have lost a good

deal. So I hope you will send the next story to me when you have it done. I'll read it right away and tell you frankly if I have any criticisms to make.[24]

Like most agents, Ober wanted to develop a reputation for offering goods that could be put into print with a minimum of editorial labor. That kind of reputation would help sell later work by the same author to the same market, and it would help sell work by other authors in the agent's stable to the market. This was an additional argument for insisting that an author channel all literary work through the agent. If a manuscript passed muster with the agent-editor, it was likely to sell more quickly and for a higher price.

Elizabeth Nowell is a good example of an agent who functioned in part as an editor. Indeed, she exercised an important editorial influence on the writing of her most famous client, Thomas Wolfe. Nowell was born in 1904 in New Bedford, Massachusetts; she graduated from Ethel Walker School in 1922 and attended Bryn Mawr on scholarship. After graduating in 1926 she took a course in writing at Columbia and published some short fiction under the pseudonym "Sarah Grinnell" in *Harper's Bazaar* and *Redbook*. In 1928 she began work as a manuscript reader at *Scribner's Magazine,* where she remained for five years, learning about both book and magazine publication during her tenure.

In 1933 she left *Scribner's* to work in Maxim Lieber's literary agency, and late that year she began to handle manuscripts by Wolfe, who had been sent to the agency by Maxwell Perkins. Wolfe was struggling to complete *Of Time and the River:* he had exhausted most of his sources of advance income and needed to publish some short fiction in periodicals in order to remain solvent. Wolfe's problem, as always, was length. Most of the promising material in his fabled trunk of manuscripts was in units of from twelve thousand to twenty thousand words—not an attractive or salable length on the periodical market. Most magazine editors wanted short stories of no more than seven or eight thousand words.

Nowell assumed the task not only of cutting these manuscripts down to marketable size, but also of training Wolfe to be a more disciplined writer. Maxwell Perkins had been pursuing the same end since 1928, with mixed results, but Perkins had been working with Wolfe on novels. The novel is an expandable form; there is no length past which it abso-

---

24. Ober to Fitzgerald, 30 August 1933, in *As Ever, Scott Fitz—Letters between F. Scott Fitzgerald and His Literary Agent Harold Ober, 1919–1940,* ed. Matthew J. Bruccoli and Jennifer McCabe Atkinson (Philadelphia: Lippincott, 1972), pp. 198–99.

lutely cannot go, and its salability is not necessarily affected by its page count. Perkins's arguments with Wolfe, his efforts to stem the flow of verbiage, could only be backed by aesthetic reasoning. Nowell had the stronger weapon of economics: Wolfe needed money and would get it only if he put his short stories into marketable length and shape.

Nowell went beyond the normal duties of an agent in her work with Wolfe. She edited his typescripts paragraph by paragraph, sometimes making block cuts, sometimes pruning within the sentence, and she gave Wolfe advice about narrative tone and descriptive detail. She understood that if magazine fiction was to sell quickly and for a good price, it needed a clearly stated or implied theme—a point the reader could readily grasp. Wolfe had a tendency to stray into autobiographical ramblings and oratorical prose, and she worked tirelessly with him to break these habits. Her method was to mark the number of words tentatively cut from each paragraph in the margin of the typescript next to that paragraph. Then she would total the marginal numbers at the bottom of each page. Wolfe usually took her advice, and eventually it had an effect on his writing. His manuscripts gradually became shorter and more compact, less autobiographical and more didactic. By 1936, Nowell no longer had to prune his work so stringently.

Wolfe's ability to adapt his work to magazine standards and Nowell's energy in marketing the manuscripts to editors yielded good income. Her first sales for him were to low-paying journals like the *American Mercury*, which purchased "Boom Town" for two hundred dollars in 1934. By 1937, however, she was having more success and was selling Wolfe's work with some regularity to the *Saturday Evening Post* and *Redbook* for fees between twelve hundred and fifteen hundred dollars. By this time she had left Lieber's agency to set up business on her own, and Wolfe had come with her. He depended on her for many personal services, especially after his break with Perkins and Scribners.[25]

Nowell was particularly useful to Wolfe in 1935 and 1936 when he took extended trips to Europe. She continued to market his writing, did his banking, and dealt with his cleaning woman. Indeed, a good agent was indispensable if an American author were planning to travel or live abroad. The talented and facile Paul Gallico, for example, was facing sub-

25. This information is taken from the introduction to Richard S. Kennedy, ed., *Beyond Love and Loyalty: The Letters of Thomas Wolfe and Elizabeth Nowell* (Chapel Hill: University of North Carolina Press, 1983).

stantial debts, a divorce, and other family problems when he escaped to England in 1936 and set about writing himself out of the red. His New York agent, Harold Ober, functioned as his unofficial banker, making payments on various debts, seeing to his life insurance, and wiring funds to him across the Atlantic. Gallico was versatile: "You know me," he wrote Ober, "I do anything for money." He was especially keen to have Ober place some of his stories with the high-paying slicks in order to "fortify the exchequer," and he proposed to Ober that they collaborate in the task of "improving the quality of belles lettres in the Satpost." The big break for Gallico came in May 1936, when Ober sold movie rights to one of Gallico's short stories to Paramount for seventy-five hundred dollars. Gallico cleared up his stateside debts and had enough money left over to purchase a cottage in South Devonshire. He was immensely grateful to Ober: "I can't tell you how fine it is to have you handling my business on the other side of the water," he wrote to the agent.[26]

One of the services provided by Ober, and by most other agents, was to keep track of the author's unsold work. The highly successful Brandt and Brandt agency kept all such manuscripts in a "B-file" for each author and looked for ways of marketing them. Early in 1941, Carl Brandt placed Stephen Vincent Benét's *Selected Works* with the Book-of-the-Month Club as a dividend selection. News of the sale spread to magazine editors, and a short story by Benét suddenly became a hot item. Brandt pulled out Benét's B-file, dusted off an unsold story called "Changing," and marketed it to the *Post* for $1,750. "I FEAR THEY ARE UNAWARE IT IS NOT FRESH FROM MILL," Brandt wired Benét, and in a later letter he admitted, "Personally, I feel a little like the cat, who has not only eaten the canary, but has had a bottle of cream all to himself!" Five months later Brandt worked the same trick again, selling a 1932 Benét B-file story entitled "Fireworks" to *Redbook* for $800.[27]

Sometimes the agent was called upon to provide story ideas for his authors. To Zona Gale, who was suffering from temporary writer's block, Paul Revere Reynolds promised, "I shall try and remember about plots and if one comes into my head which I think will interest you, I shall

26. The Gallico-Ober correspondence is in Box 1, Ober Associates Collection, Columbia University. Quotations from Gallico to Ober, 25 February, 2 April, 22 May, and 11 December 1936.

27. Benét Papers, Beinecke Library, Yale University. Quotations from Carl Brandt to Benét, 21 February 1941 (cable) and 24 February 1941.

certainly let you have it."[28] Reynolds did similar duty for Ida Tarbell, funneling article ideas to her from various magazine editors; Harold Ober did the same for Gallico. On occasion these instructions were quite specific, even covering structure and tone. Some authors, however, refused to work under such conditions. Booth Tarkington, for example, specifically asked Reynolds not to relay ideas to him from magazine editors, nor did Tarkington like it when these same editors, communicating through Reynolds, offered large prices for unwritten work. The anticipation of so many dollars caused his pen to run dry.

An agent could be useful to the author in dealing with a former publisher. Such business could be awkward, especially if the parting had been acrimonious. After leaving Maxwell Perkins and Scribners, for example, Conrad Aiken did not have to correspond with the firm about the few remaining business details; his agent Bernice Baumgarten at Brandt and Brandt handled those chores. Baumgarten performed a similar service for Benét, effecting the release from Henry Holt of Benét's first two books and transferring all rights and printing plates to Farrar and Rinehart, Benét's new publisher. This sort of negotiation became much more difficult, however, as the author's output grew. The dealings that took place whenever Theodore Dreiser changed publishers during the last years of his career, for example, were labyrinthine and always expensive for the new publisher.

Most American publishers eventually realized that literary agents could be useful—that they could take over many time-consuming duties for the editor. Agents came to function more and more as editors had once functioned. They answered mail, secured books and research materials, performed errands, renewed copyrights, and assisted authors with their tax returns. Indeed the functions of the editor and the agent eventually became almost identical, and many persons moved easily from one position to the other. The only real adjustment was to transfer one's primary loyalty from author to publishing house or vice versa. Some persons even managed to free-lance or work part-time simultaneously in both capacities. Book publishers and magazine editors also learned that they could rely on certain agents for material. Eventually some publishing houses and periodical editors ceased to consider manuscripts that came in over the transom and dealt only with agents. The *Saturday Evening Post*, for

28. Reynolds to Gale, 1 July 1933, P. R. Reynolds Papers.

example, paid a weekly call to Paul Revere Reynolds to pick up material by his authors that *he* thought might interest them.

Editors at publishing houses also learned that agents could serve as buffers. Ideally, trade editors should not be overly direct in making criticisms to promising young authors, but they can be straightforward with agents, who have much less emotion and ego at stake. Thus editor Robert Linscott at Random House could be frank with Berta Kaslow of the William Morris agency about Norman Mailer's first attempt at a novel, a manuscript entitled "A Transit to Narcissus." The book showed promise, wrote Linscott, but exhibited "no organization, no structure, no restraint." The "motivation is cloudy," continued Linscott, and the writing "exceedingly verbose."[29] Linscott could count on Kaslow, who knew Mailer's personality better than he, to tone down such comments if she thought them too blunt.

Authors eventually recognized the virtual necessity of employing literary agents. The agent, who often had some training in law and accounting, could examine publishers' contracts and royalty statements for hidden clauses or mathematical errors. Agents were indispensable in dealing with the bureaucracy and inefficiency of large trade publishing firms. The agent was usually a better negotiator than the author and often had a better notion of the monetary value of a manuscript. An agent could arrange for houses to bid against one another for an author's work or even auction the manuscript to the highest bidder. These were thought to be unethical practices for an author but were considered acceptable for an agent. The agent could function as the author's banker, taking royalty and magazine receipts, paying off creditors, doling out funds from a reserve account, and advancing money on unwritten or unsold work. It is not surprising, therefore, that many authors came to feel more loyalty toward their agents than toward their editors or publishers. Especially today, when editors' jobs are apt to depend on the profits shown by the books they bring in, authors are inclined to ally themselves more closely to their agents. The agent, one presumes, will always be there; the editor may be gone tomorrow.

Literary scholars who work with authors' papers almost invariably notice that author-agent correspondence differs in tone from author-editor correspondence. The editor represents a business that pays money to the

29. Linscott to Kaslow, 17 April 1944, Box 94, Random House Papers.

author, or means to, and the author, however illogically, sees the editor as a kind of employer. By contrast, the author is the employer of the agent; the agent's fee comes from the author's pocket, and the author can be more authoritative with an agent than with an editor. Authors often feel closer to their agents than to their editors, and the tone of their letters is accordingly more casual, sometimes even intimate. Author-editor correspondence is typically more formal on both sides.

The agent serves a useful psychological purpose. By ridding the author-publisher relationship of the taint of business, the agent leaves the author and editor free to discuss artistic and aesthetic matters without a residue of ill feeling from prior contract negotiations. To put it more bluntly, the agent is someone on whom both the author and the publisher can blame their greed. If contract negotiations have been difficult, and if the publisher has had to make many concessions, the author can explain that the agent was to blame for the holdout. The publisher may in fact have been parsimonious in the original offer, and the agent may only have brought pressure to force an agreement to reasonable terms, but the publisher, too, can blame the delay on the agent. The publisher and the author understand, of course, that the agent is simply reflecting greed (or niggardliness) on both sides, but neither one need admit that fact. The editing, production, and selling of the book can proceed without rancor. On the question of literary agents, there is a great difference between what people say and what they believe. The agent must simply learn to accept this shifting of blame as a drawback of the occupation.[30]

During the 1890s and early 1900s, literary agents in the United States functioned primarily as intermediaries between magazine and book publishers in England and America. They scouted for material on behalf of English publishers and tried to place English writing (published and unpublished) on the American market. However, with the enormous growth of the magazine industry in America after 1900, agents began to work primarily as brokers who offered the writings of their clients to magazine editors and who fielded offers made by those editors to their clients. Agents also handled negotiations between authors and book publishers, and they began to take over some of the routine chores that had

---

30. A recent, frank memoir by a literary agent is Helen M. Strauss, *A Talent for Luck: An Autobiography* (New York: Random House, 1979). An interesting novel, written from the narrative point of view of a literary agent, is Richard Marek's *Works of Genius* (New York: Atheneum, 1987). Marek is president and publisher of E. P. Dutton.

formerly fallen to trade editors. After World War I, agents became increasingly involved with subsidiary rights. It became the agent's most important duty to recycle a client's writings, to make them yield income repeatedly over a period of years through various forms of republication, adaptation, and performance. Indeed, that is the major business of an agent today, especially when representing an author who hopes, however quixotically, to survive on literary earnings alone.

Chapter 6

The Magazine Market

It's all a question of how much a writer can stand to compromise.

—Elizabeth Nowell to Vardis Fisher (1935)

During the 1880s and 1890s, modern mass-circulation magazines came into being in the United States. For the author they provided an important outlet for work and a major source of income. Before 1880, serious authors had only a few respectable magazines in which they could publish—*Scribner's, Harper's,* the *Century,* and three or four others. Such magazines were usually allied with book publishing firms and addressed a relatively well-educated and genteel audience. They tended, in editorial philosophy, to pattern themselves after such British models as *Blackwood's,* the *Edinburgh Review,* and the *Fortnightly.* In the 1890s and early 1900s, however, editors and publishers like Frank Munsey, S. S. McClure, John Brisben Walker, Edward Bok, and George Horace Lorimer began to produce mass-circulation magazines for a vast middle-to-lowbrow American readership that hitherto had not been addressed successfully. Advances in printing technology—especially in the reproduction of illustrations—made it possible to manufacture visually attractive magazines in huge printing runs and to price them at fifteen cents or a dime, well within reach of these new audiences. During this same period, America was making the final transition from a largely agricultural economy to a predominantly industrial one. Urbanization, growth in average income, better public education, and an increase in leisure time combined to produce a ready audience for magazines that published popular fiction and articles of general interest. During the first half of the twentieth century the American author could publish stories and serialize novels in an unprecedented number and variety of such magazines.

The great boom in national retailing and the growing importance of brand names made mass-circulation magazines the ideal advertising medium for American business. Indeed, it was the partnership between advertising and magazines that made possible the enormous growth of the periodical industry in the United States. Magazine publishers could sell their magazines for less than production costs and still take substantial profits from advertising revenues. Magazine publishers thus became intermediaries between specific groups of businessmen and homogeneous groups of readers. A publisher had to devise an editorial philosophy that would appeal to a particular body of readers and acquire material to fit that philosophy. Then space had to be sold to advertisers who wanted to present their products to that segment of the retail market. Almost every magazine was designed for a well-defined public, large or small, within the total population. As a consequence, the magazine publisher came to be a dealer both in reading matter and in consumer groups.

The great success of magazines such as the *Saturday Evening Post, Ladies' Home Journal, Redbook, Munsey's, Collier's, Woman's Home Companion,* the *Delineator, Cosmopolitan, McCall's, Liberty,* the various McClure publications, and many other magazines opened up high-paying markets for fiction writers and began to make the services of a good literary agent indispensable. Agents became brokers between magazines and authors, guiding writers to editors who could use their work and introducing editors to authors whose writing would fit the needs of their magazines. Not coincidentally, advertising agencies began to spring up in New York and in other publishing centers at about this time. Such agencies facilitated dealings at another "interface": they brought businesses in touch with magazines that would reach their particular markets, helped these businesses with copy-writing and layout, and carried out elementary experiments in market analysis.[1]

The important role played by advertising in the magazine industry had an effect on content. A magazine like the *Smart Set,* which addressed a limited and sophisticated readership, could afford to be risqué or controversial because it charged a high price per copy and did not court advertising from name-brand national firms. The drawback for the author was that the *Smart Set* and other magazines of its kind paid low fees—from one hundred to four hundred dollars for a short story and even less for nonfiction. Writers who wanted to publish in mass-circulation magazines and enjoy the financial rewards and wide exposure of such publication had to be ready to tailor their work for those markets. That usually meant turning out a relatively bland product. Much of the material in mass-

1. Theodore Peterson, *Magazines in the Twentieth Century,* 2d ed. (Urbana: University of Illinois Press, 1964), chaps. 1–5; James Playsted Wood, *Magazines in the United States,* 2d ed. (New York: Ronald Press, 1956), chaps. 9–11, 13, 20–21.

circulation magazines was written to order. Experienced authors like John P. Marquand and Eric Ambler would receive specific instructions from editors about subject matter, structure, tone, and length. The editor might even dictate the point of the article, story, or poem; the author would write to these specifications for an agreed-upon price, negotiated by the agent.

One writer who worked well within this system was Booth Tarkington, who for over thirty years received top prices for his short fiction and serials from national magazines—particularly from the *Saturday Evening Post.* The editorial philosophy of the *Post* was pro-business and pro-success. The hero of a typical *Post* story used his inborn resourcefulness to overcome difficulties and to achieve high standing in business and fulfillment in love. This philosophy originated in the personal beliefs of George Horace Lorimer, editor of the magazine, who liked to call himself "The Old Hard-Boiled Self-Made Merchant." Few deviations from pattern were allowed in the *Post,* and an author had to be willing to conform in order to publish there.[2]

Most of the stories Tarkington submitted to the *Post* were readily and even enthusiastically accepted, and Lorimer regularly raised Tarkington's story fee in order to bind him more securely to the magazine. By 1939, Tarkington's price had reached four thousand dollars per story. The self-effacing Gentleman from Indiana was so embarrassed by Lorimer's generosity that he asked, in January 1939, to have his price *cut*—a suggestion that Lorimer laughed down. Tarkington sometimes had to alter his work for the *Post,* however. Political themes, for example, were verboten: the *Post* returned Tarkington's story "Ripley, Try to Be Nice" in April 1939 because "it is patent anti-New Deal propaganda and we have burnt our fingers on propaganda stories." Tarkington removed the political references and sold the manuscript to the *Post* on a second try.[3]

2. John Tebbel, *George Horace Lorimer and the* Saturday Evening Post (Garden City, N.Y.: Doubleday, 1948); "George Horace Lorimer," in James Playsted Wood, *The Curtis Magazines* (New York: Ronald Press, 1971). In 1901–2, Lorimer wrote an extraordinarily popular epistolary series for the *Post* entitled "Letters from a Self-made Merchant to His Son"—hence the sobriquet. Also see Bernard Berelson and Patricia J. Salter, "Majority and Minority Americans: An Analysis of Magazine Fiction," *Public Opinion Quarterly* 10 (1946): 168–90; and Patricke Johns-Heine and Hans H. Gerth, "Values in Mass Periodical Fiction, 1921–1940," *Public Opinion Quarterly* 13 (1949): 105–13.

3. Adelaide W. Neall (*Post* fiction editor) to Tarkington, 17 April 1939, Tarkington Papers, Princeton University, Princeton, N.J. Literary feuding was also not allowed. In March 1930, Sherwood Anderson sent an article on cotton-mill workers to John Hall Wheelock at *Scribner's Magazine.* The manuscript, entitled "Labor and Sinclair Lewis," was

Near the end of his life, Tarkington's fiction—heretofore relentlessly upbeat—began to take on slightly darker tones. His novel *The Man of the Family* was turned down for serialization by the *Post* in February 1940 because fiction editor Adelaide W. Neall thought it "very depressing reading, and it is the fact that it is depressing up to the end that makes us doubt it as a serial for a popular magazine." For almost the first time in the long history of his dealings with the *Post,* Tarkington was moved to protest. Correspondence followed with Neall about such subjects as "reality" and "life," but she was not persuaded. "I am not prepared to argue with you when you say that none of our lives has a happy ending," she wrote him. Then she added with incontrovertible commercial logic: "Isn't that perhaps why people want to read stories that suggest that perhaps some of the characters are going to find happiness?" Tarkington gave in and by early March 1940 was revising his serial. He still retained his imaginative facility and his knack for compromise; on 18 March, Neall accepted the revised novel for publication. In her congratulatory letter she told Tarkington, with no apparent irony: "We have all been admiring the seemingly effortless skill with which you have repaired the weaknesses—from a serial point of view—in MAN OF THE FAMILY." Neall was not quite finished with the novel, however. When she sent galleys to Tarkington in April, she directed that he cut "hells or damns or other swear words," all of which she had queried in the margins. He could have a few, she noted, but only a few.[4]

Even a willingness to compromise would not always guarantee a sale, especially if the material in a prospective serial involved a woman of doubtful moral behavior. Zona Gale's novel *Light Woman* dealt with an actress who refused to marry the man with whom she had been living because, after the fashion of the time, she was opposed to the idea of marriage. The manuscript had another drawback as well—it contained a suicide. *Ladies' Home Journal* turned down *Light Woman* in 1934 as did *Cosmopolitan,* even after Gale had offered to change her ending and have her heroine marry the man. Edwin Balmer at *Redbook* stalled, then asked

---

in part an attack on the author of *Main Street* for his satirical portraits of life in small American towns. Wheelock found Anderson's treatment of Lewis too vehement and personal and required Anderson to rewrite in order to direct his criticisms more generally against a group of anti-small-town writers. (Wheelock to Anderson, 19 March 1930, Scribner Archive, Princeton University, Princeton, N.J.)

4. Neall to Tarkington, 12 and 19 February, 18 March, and 22 April 1940, Tarkington Papers, Princeton University, Princeton, N.J.

for a new ending; Gale rewrote her conclusion, but Balmer still rejected *Light Woman*. Through Paul Revere Reynolds the novel was offered in succession to *Woman's Home Companion, Pictorial Weekly, Harper's, Scribner's, McCall's,* the *Delineator, Collier's,* and even the *New York Herald Tribune,* which sometimes printed first-run serials. At that point, Reynolds gave up and returned the manuscript to Gale, who, through a friend, played a long shot and sent the novel to *Liberty*. That magazine, to Gale's great relief, bought the serial rights. Gale had learned a hard lesson about the kind of behavior expected of heroines in popular magazine fiction.[5]

Money from the magazines was extremely important to writers before 1940. Indeed, they often made a good deal more from serial rights than from book royalties. Between 1919 and 1936, F. Scott Fitzgerald earned some $225,784 for his magazine fiction as opposed to only $66,588 for his novels. Theodore Dreiser, in the early 1920s, was still relying heavily on fees for magazine work to meet his day-to-day expenses. Dreiser was by then in his early fifties and was the author of five novels, including *Sister Carrie, Jennie Gerhardt,* and *The Financier,* but those books brought him little in the way of dependable income. And Edith Wharton, to take one final example, left Scribners for Appleton in part because the latter house offered more profitable arrangements for serializing her novels in magazines.[6] Serial money, collected in advance, could make it possible to complete a book. A dependable writer whose work was in demand could often contract for serial rights on the basis of a manuscript that was only about one-fourth complete. If an editor liked the finished chapters and the accompanying synopsis of the rest of the story, the magazine would buy the serial rights for a stated figure, payable in installments. An advance of perhaps one-third of the money would be made initially. The author lived on these funds while composing subsequent chapters and collected further checks as later chapters were delivered against specific deadlines. Often the early chapters were running in the magazine before the final chapters had been composed. When these last chapters were de-

5. Zona Gale files, P. R. Reynolds Papers, Butler Library, Columbia University, New York, esp. Reynolds to Gale, 6 September 1934.

6. *As Ever, Scott Fitz—Letters between F. Scott Fitzgerald and His Literary Agent Harold Ober, 1919–1940,* ed. Matthew J. Bruccoli and Jennifer McCabe Atkinson (Philadelphia: Lippincott, 1972), p. xviii; Thomas P. Riggio's introduction to Dreiser's *American Diaries, 1920–1926,* ed. Thomas P. Riggio et al. (Philadelphia: University of Pennsylvania Press, 1982), p. 15; Charles A. Madison, "Charles Scribner and Edith Wharton," in *Irving to Irving: Author-Publisher Relations, 1800–1974* (New York: Bowker, 1974), pp. 140–41.

livered, the author received the remainder of the money and was free to begin revising the novel for book publication.

Frequently, however, the author had to pay an artistic price for serial publication. Some novels lend themselves more readily to serialization than others: an episodic story with a chronologically arranged plot, for example, can easily be presented in coherent segments over a five- or six-month period. On the other hand, a novel written within a twenty-four-hour time frame or a narrative with frequent flashbacks and dislocations in chronology will not appear to best advantage in monthly installments. *A Farewell to Arms,* for example, is a relatively straightforward narrative; it was a simple matter for *Scribner's Magazine* to serialize the book in six segments from May to October of 1929. *Tender Is the Night,* by contrast, has a complex time frame and employs a major flashback sequence that takes up the middle third of the book. By splitting this three-part novel into four installments, *Scribner's Magazine* made the potentially confusing narrative structure quite difficult to follow. Fitzgerald was convinced that most reviewers of *Tender* had read it as a serial and that they had gotten a negative first impression of the book in that medium.

Authors who were interested in selling serial rights obviously needed to write their novels with serialization in mind from the beginning, taking care to structure the narrative in installments suitable for monthly magazine publication. James Boyd's first novel, a historical adventure about the Revolutionary War entitled *Drums,* had not been written in this fashion, however, and Robert Bridges, editor of *Scribner's Magazine,* turned it down for magazine publication in 1924 because of Boyd's technique of delineating character. "The very excellence of your method which reproduces the character through a succession of episodes, rather than through the development of a strong story, seems to me to stand in the way of that impelling interest which is necessary in a serial," wrote Bridges to the young author. In composing subsequent novels, Boyd took care to tailor his manuscripts for the serial market. For example, when he sent the first installment of *Roll River* to Maxwell Perkins ten years later, he noted: "The action is sustained, and the break is logical. I have an idea that the succeeding installments will not only be briefer but more rapid in movement and therefore satisfactory from a serialization standpoint."[7]

Concessions to taste and decorum also had to be made. *Scribner's*

---

7. Bridges to Boyd, 13 May 1924; Boyd to Perkins, 20 March 1934, Scribner Archive. In his letter to Perkins, Boyd refers to *Roll River* by its working title, "The Dark Shore."

Magazine had to persuade Hemingway to omit numerous words and lines from *A Farewell to Arms* because they were judged too strong for magazine presentation.[8] Pregnancy, even within wedlock, was a delicate subject: Fitzgerald's 1926 novella "The Rich Boy" was made fit for appearance in *Redbook* by a bumbling editor who removed from the text, without Fitzgerald's permission, all references to the character Paula Hagerty's swollen shape during her pregnancy. One can imagine the confusion in readers' minds when Paula dies in childbirth a few pages later, without its having been mentioned that she is with child. By 1939 Fitzgerald had learned to anticipate such problems. While drafting *The Last Tycoon,* he realized that some of his material would be potentially censorable. He wrote Kenneth Littauer, editor of *Collier's,* that he would compose the central seduction scene two ways: "Now we have a love affair between Stahr and Thalia, an immediate, dynamic, unusual, physical love affair—and I will write it so that you can publish it. At the same time I will send you a copy of how it will appear in book form somewhat stronger in tone."[9]

Some authors saw serialization as undignified. Ellen Glasgow, who was much concerned about her literary reputation, all but forbade her agent Paul Revere Reynolds from offering serial rights for her novels to mass-circulation magazines.[10] More business-minded authors simply saw serialization as a source of additional income. In answer to a query from agent Carl Brandt about a serial feeler from England, John P. Marquand sent a simple two-word telegram: "HOW MUCH?" An author, however, often lost some control over the text in return for serial money. After purchasing North American serial rights to Marquand's *Point of No Return* for sixty thousand dollars, *Ladies' Home Journal* made it clear to Brandt that some cutting and editorial rewriting might be done. "It is understood," they wrote, "that we must of necessity be the final judges as to what goes into the magazine."[11] Even when novels had been written to specifications, authors could end up with maimed texts, especially if

8. Michael S. Reynolds, *Hemingway's First War: The Making of* A Farewell to Arms (Princeton: Princeton University Press, 1976), chap. 3.

9. James L. W. West III and J. Barclay Inge, "F. Scott Fitzgerald's Revision of 'The Rich Boy'," *Proof* 5 (1976): 133; Fitzgerald to Littauer, 29 September 1939, *Correspondence of F. Scott Fitzgerald,* ed. Matthew J. Bruccoli and Margaret M. Duggan (New York: Random House, 1980), p. 547.

10. James B. Colvert, ed., "Agent and Author: Ellen Glasgow's Letters to Paul Revere Reynolds," *Studies in Bibliography* 14 (1961): 177–96.

11. Marquand to Brandt (cable), 7 December 1948; Hugh M. Kahler (*Ladies' Home Journal*) to Carl Brandt, 21 September 1948, Marquand Collection, Beinecke Library, Yale University, New Haven, Conn.

they were not close enough to New York to oversee publication. In 1921, English novelist Arnold Bennett wrote angrily from London to Eric Schuler of the Authors League that the *Delineator* had butchered the first four serial installments of *Mr. Prohack,* a one-hundred-thousand-word novel that he had written for the magazine, as directed, in seven installments of some fourteen thousand words each. From the first four installments, totaling fifty-seven thousand words, the *Delineator* had cut more than twenty-six thousand words. Bennett was furious, but there was nothing he could do.[12] A year later, Fitzgerald's second novel, *The Beautiful and Damned,* was treated similarly by Carl Hovey at *Metropolitan Magazine.* Fitzgerald was unhappy, but the only satisfaction he received was in seeing the uncut text published in book form by Scribners after the serial run was over.[13]

Authors who wrote regularly for mass-circulation magazines sometimes found themselves typecast by previous material. After the great success of her two-volume *Early Life of Abraham Lincoln* in 1900, Ida Tarbell found that there was virtually no way she could *stop* writing about Lincoln, so insistent were magazine editors that she do follow-up articles on incidents from his life that she had not treated in her biography. People who had known Lincoln or had observed him would contact her with requests that she write up this or that incident; sometimes Tarbell would pay a percentage of her magazine fee to the source of the material. She probably could have made her way easily for the rest of her career by manufacturing little else but spin-off articles on Lincoln, but she very much wanted to work with different material. So eager was she to write on other subjects that she proposed to Reynolds a lengthy article on "the rise of the hookless fastener"—to us, the zipper. It was a "rather long and dramatic story," she assured him.[14]

Stephen Vincent Benét's short story "The Devil and Daniel Webster," published first in the *Saturday Evening Post* on 24 October 1936, brought wide notice to its author and was quickly anthologized in numerous high school textbooks. The story was also adapted for radio and the movies; later a stage play and a television production were mounted. Benét found a ready market thereafter for short fiction based on incidents in American

12. Bennett to Schuler, 14 October 1921, Authors League file, Henry Holt Papers, Princeton University, Princeton, N.J.

13. See Arthur Mizener, *The Far Side of Paradise,* rev. ed. (Boston: Houghton Mifflin, 1965), p. 158.

14. Tarbell to Reynolds, 22 August 1927, P. R. Reynolds Papers.

history, but eventually he tired of the material. He complained in a letter to his agent, Carl Brandt, and asked that Brandt try to interest magazine editors in something else. Brandt, however, did not seem to understand the problem: "I am much interested in the spread of your patriotic writing," he wrote Benét. "In all seriousness, I don't see how you can get out of it or think you should."[15] Still, Benét felt trapped by his own success with "Daniel Webster."

Something similar happened to William Faulkner in his dealings with *Scribner's Magazine* during the early 1930s. Faulkner sold a cut-down version of "Spotted Horses" to *Scribner's* in February 1931 and thereafter had difficulty selling them anything else for a time, so determined were they to have another Flem Snopes story. K. C. Crichton, assistant editor of the magazine, wrote Faulkner, "We regret that it has not been possible to accept more of the stories you have offered us, but on Flem Snopes we are clear. He is our character and we think that in your hands he will become one of the great characters of literature." Faulkner was probably flattered, but unfortunately for *Scribner's* he had found a higher-paying market for his Flem Snopes material—the *Saturday Evening Post*. In the meantime he sent other stories to *Scribner's*, including "Rose of Lebanon," "Idyll in the Desert," and "All the Dead Pilots," but all were turned down. "We have become so hipped on the thought of Flem Snopes," wrote Crichton, "that we are confining all our prayers in the hope that George Horace Lorimer will be struck with lightning just at the time those pieces of yours reach him."[16]

Fitzgerald must have felt similarly trapped in 1937 when, down on his luck and living in a seedy hotel in Tryon, North Carolina, he was desperately attempting to manufacture amusing love stories, in his old style, for the *Post*. Fitzgerald was heavily in debt to Charles Scribner's Sons, his publisher, and to Harold Ober, his literary agent. He had been in debt before—indeed, it was almost a perpetual condition for him after 1920—but he had always been able to rescue himself by writing short fiction for the *Post* and other mass-circulation magazines. In fact he had even tried to have himself declared "virtually an employee" of the *Post* in 1932 for income tax purposes.[17] By 1937, however, Fitzgerald had lost the knack of

15. Brandt to Benét, 27 June 1941, Benét Collection, Beinecke Library, Yale University, New Haven, Conn.

16. Crichton to Faulkner, 23 July and 6 August 1931, in James B. Meriwether, ed., "Faulkner's Correspondence with *Scribner's Magazine*," *Proof* 3 (1973): 268–69.

17. Fitzgerald to Ober, ca. 21 April 1932, *As Ever, Scott Fitz—*, pp. 190–93.

turning out salable material for the popular fiction market. This situation was caused in part by his inability to write convincingly about his proto-typical Fitzgerald heroine. Young, beautiful, and willfully independent, she had been a feature of nearly all of his magazine fiction since 1919. By 1937, however, Fitzgerald was no longer much interested in her, and his repeated attempts to recreate her in his post-1935 stories were unsuccessful. These stories are puzzling: the familiar matter of his earlier *Post* fiction is there, but the manner is lacking. The heroines are curiously diminished versions of their more engaging, vital sisters from Fitzgerald's earlier stories. As a working author, however, he had to meet the demands of his market, which, as he interpreted it, still wanted his heroine.

In March 1937, living in the Tryon hotel, the weary Fitzgerald began a story of young love entitled "A Full Life." The manuscript opened with an improbable incident in which his heroine, named Gwen Davis, donned an inflatable flying suit and floated out the window of a Manhattan skyscraper. This was to be the first occurrence of a motif Fitzgerald wanted to work into the story, a motif of flying and falling. Gwen flies and falls first from the skyscraper window, later from the deck of an ocean liner, and finally from a circus cannon. Had he been able to inject his writing with a suitably light tone, Fitzgerald might have brought off this little fantasy, but as one reads through the surviving draft of the story, one sees that his heart was not in the work. Plotting is artificial, characters are wooden, and motivations are unclear.

About midway through the draft, Fitzgerald apparently realized what was happening and, in disgust, worked a freakish detail into the story. He quite literally filled his heroine with dynamite. Gwen leaves her childhood home because she does not want to "raise the roof." Later she marries the son of a gunpowder manufacturer because she has "always belonged to him." Still later she becomes a circus daredevil who makes her living by being shot from a cannon. Gwen's performing name is symptomatic of Fitzgerald's dislike for her: he dubs her "The Human Shell"—and indeed she is an empty character. Discouraged by his inability to bring his dynamite-filled heroine to life and tired of trying to manufacture yet another light romance for the *Post,* Fitzgerald made a macabre private gesture in his manuscript. He blew Gwen up. The explosion killed a man standing next to her and was heard as far away as New York City. This grisly little tale reveals much about Fitzgerald's state of mind during his famous Crack-Up period. He felt victimized by his previous success, locked into writing one kind of story about one type of character—a heroine about whom he no longer cared.[18]

Many authors of novels and short fiction chafed under the formal and structural limitations imposed on them by mass-circulation magazines. They disliked the simplistic, undeviating pattern of the "formula" story: it began typically with action or dialogue in order to capture the attention of a reader paging through an issue; it was rigidly plotted and moved relentlessly toward an artificial climax; and it ended with a "final suspiration," often faintly saccharine in tone, usually in the advertising pages at the rear of the magazine.[19] Some writers (Sherwood Anderson, for example) could not adapt to these limitations. Other authors— Fitzgerald, Faulkner, and Dreiser among them—learned to work more or less within the formula and eventually turned out some very good short fiction for the big-audience slicks. Writing for high-paying magazines, however, was not a predictable business. Editors and staff readers changed with some frequency at the various magazines, and editorial requirements fluctuated. Writing for the magazines took patience, adaptability, and a thick skin. There was no sheet of dos and don'ts for prospective authors to follow; length, subject matter, tone, language, plot, characterization—all had to be negotiated by a complicated system of trial and error, inference and suggestion, submission, rejection, and resubmission. The work could be frustrating, but the potential financial rewards were large. In fact, most American authors before World War I saw the magazine market as virtually their only source of big money. After the war, however, different ways of publishing one's work, or adapting it to other media, began to emerge. Books could be serialized or abridged or distributed through book clubs or reprinted as paperbacks; story material could be adapted for presentation on the radio, stage, screen, or lecture circuit. Even translation rights could yield significant amounts of money for some books. The author set about tapping these new sources of income and learning how to exploit the full earning potential of what was now beginning to be called a "literary property."

18. See James L. W. West III, "Fitzgerald Explodes His Heroine," *Princeton University Library Chronicle* 49 (1988): 159–65.
19. Henry Seidel Canby, "Free Fiction," *Atlantic Monthly* 116 (July 1915): 60–68.

Chapter 7

Subsidiary Rights

> But the novelist—and one speaks now of the American—
> may sell the same work over many times.
>
> —Frank Norris (1902)

American authors during the twentieth century have had to recycle their work. That is to say, they and their agents have had to discover ways of exploiting fully the subsidiary or ancillary rights that attach to literary property. These are the rights for republication or representation of the text in other forms, for adaptation of the material to other media, and for reuse of the characters in other story lines. A piece of writing—a short story, poem, novel, or essay—ideally should be made to generate income over a period of years, after the initial act of composition has been completed. The success or failure of an author's career in financial terms has often depended on how well this principle has been mastered. Labor on a manuscript must be regarded by the author as an investment. Will the published literary work yield short-term returns only, or will it produce income over a long period? There are advantages to both types of publication, but most authors, given a choice, would probably take the latter. The best thing, of course, is to produce work that pays both ways—with immediate popular success and large initial sales and with subsequent income from other forms of publication, adaptation, or performance.

American authors have attempted to realize money on the ancillary rights to their work almost from the beginnings of literary publication in the United States. Their first efforts to exploit these rights, however, were hindered by an underdeveloped publishing trade. Literary work published before 1790 in the United States went automatically into the public domain, and if it had commercial value it was immediately pirated and sold by other domestic printer-publishers. The U.S. copyright law of 1790 was a small beginning: it afforded protection for only fourteen years (later renewable for fourteen more), and it could be enforced only in this country, but it did give the status of property to works of the imagination. In the early days of the republic, however, there were few ways in which a work of literature could be recycled. The act of publication, in economic terms, was usually a one-time affair. The market was not large enough or well enough developed to yield long-term sales for any but the most successful works of literature—popular novels like Mrs. Susanna Rowson's best-seller *Charlotte Temple,* first published in the United States in 1794. Thus Fenimore Cooper had to produce lengthy new novels regularly in order to satisfy his audience and generate dependable income. Cooper and Washington Irving were both able to republish their work in second and third editions, but stereotype plating was not yet widespread in America, and each book had to be reset in standing type before republication. For the printer-publisher, this made second and third editions identical in economic terms to first editions, and it discouraged the production of large collected-edition sets for the marginally popular author.

Henry Wadsworth Longfellow was probably the first American author to exploit successfully the subsidiary rights to his work. In fact, his astuteness as a literary businessman helped make it possible for him to retire from college teaching in 1854 at the age of forty-seven and live in large part off the proceeds of his pen for the remainder of his life. Longfellow's approach was sound. For periodical publication, he sold off the first serial rights to his poems. Then every few years he published clothbound collections of his poems, most of which had already appeared in magazines or annuals. Long narratives in verse, such as *Evangeline* (1847) and *The Courtship of Miles Standish* (1858), were published as separate volumes. Longfellow revised his work for collected appearances, and he spent some time and creative thought in arranging the sequence of poems in each new volume, but the original imaginative acts that had produced the poems did not have to be duplicated. The work of art was thus made to generate two types of income—a fixed fee for its periodical appearance and a percentage of the profits on the clothbound collection.

Longfellow's collections were popular enough to be reprinted. Apparently he had envisioned this possibility years earlier, for he had taken the precaution of paying personally for the typesetting and plating of his separate collections. Thus he had assumed a larger portion of the risk of publication and had been able to negotiate a higher percentage of the profits from his publishers. He had also retained ownership of the plates (which American printers were by then using), and when it came time to issue more copies, he simply had the books reprinted from these plates. The savings in production costs were significant. There were no new charges for composing—an important economy. In economic terms, these reprints were therefore more profitable than the first editions had been. In 1845, when he had produced several separate collections of verse, Longfellow decided to bring out a large collection entitled *Poems*. He did the same thing with his prose works in 1857. These collected editions sold well, especially as gift books—an approximate equivalent to our coffee-table books today.

During all this time Longfellow continued to write new poetry. He published some single poems in periodicals or annuals, as he always had done, and every few years he republished those poems, with other new ones, in single-volume collections. Longfellow saw that there were different markets for his poetry, and he addressed these in different formats. For the carriage trade he had his publisher manufacture deluxe editions, printed on heavy paper, illustrated and bound handsomely. For the middle-range buyer and for the library, his publisher produced sturdy books bound in cloth. These editions offered identical texts, printed from the same plates, but they sold to different segments of the market. For the lowest portion of the trade Longfellow had his poems reset, at his own expense, in a closely packed, double-column format, and he had this edition marketed as the equivalent of a paperback today—a flimsy, pamphlet-like fascicle that sold for fifty cents. Longfellow's writings did quite well in all of these formats. Later, in 1866, he was able to issue a revised and enlarged collected edition of his poetry, also in several formats. He knew that his writings had broad popular appeal, and he took care to make them available to readers at all levels.[1]

In 1832 Ralph Waldo Emerson decided to become a full-time man of letters. His decision took courage: he was giving up a respected position and a steady income as a Unitarian minister and was entering an occupation that carried no real social status and was precarious economically. Emerson's first years as a writer and lecturer were lean, but eventually he did well. Like Longfellow, he learned to recycle his work, though his method of doing so was different.

Most students of American literature believe that Emerson was at his best in his journals. His most memorable ideas are nearly all found in

1. William Charvat, "Longfellow" and "Longfellow's Income from His Writings, 1842–1852," *The Profession of Authorship in America, 1800–1870* (Columbus: Ohio State University Press, 1968), pp. 106–67.

short passages embedded in his private notebooks. He developed into a journal keeper in part because of the way in which he earned his living. He gained his steadiest income as a traveling lecturer, and his schedule was hectic, particularly during the early years of his literary career. He had no lecture agent to negotiate his fees, arrange for his transportation, or book his hotel room. These matters he handled himself, and much of his energy and time was absorbed by them. Because Emerson found it difficult to reserve regular hours for composition, he had to develop a method better suited to the pace of his life. He learned to concentrate his thinking and writing into brief periods and to record the results in his journals. These journals had no immediate commercial value, but Emerson mined them constantly, transferring material from them into his lectures. According to contemporary witnesses, Emerson's presentations on the circuit were brilliant but disorganized. Often they seemed to be composed of one memorable passage followed by another and then another until the alloted time was up. Frequently Emerson finished the hour only halfway through his stack of notes, but in these notes he had been polishing the best passages from his journals. Oral presentation was giving him an opportunity to hear them with his own ear and to experiment with them on a live audience. The lectures could be revised, reordered, and presented again and again. Emerson's lecture fees in the early years of his career were low—often he traveled many miles for ten dollars—but later he regularly received fifty dollars plus expenses for a lecture, a good sum in those days. The important point, however, is that a lecture required no fresh invention. Emerson could create and imagine in his private journals as his schedule allowed. His best ideas could then be transferred from the journals to the lectures and, eventually, after more reordering and polishing, could become parts of published essays.

Emerson earned little from the sale of his writings in printed form, but that was largely the fault of his various publishers. Emerson insisted for most of his career on issuing his writings through Boston publishers. These firms traditionally did business on a very small scale and, after the European fashion, preferred to concentrate on a geographically limited market—Boston and a few surrounding towns. Emerson's writings had potential appeal for a much wider reading audience, but during his lifetime he never reached it. Money from the sale of his books was never substantial or dependable, and Emerson consequently hesitated to put his essays into print. Once he had published certain passages and ideas, he was reluctant to continue using them in his lectures. They were his best source of steady income, and he had to keep them fresh.[2]

Of the Realists who flourished after the Civil War, William Dean Howells probably exploited his ancillary rights most effectively. Howells was active in the magazine and book worlds as an editor, columnist, and novelist, and he was in an excellent position to make use of the machinery of the literary marketplace. Nearly all of his mature novels were serialized before book publication; often they appeared in one of the periodicals published by Harper and Brothers—either *Harper's Monthly* or *Harper's Bazaar*—or in a magazine like the *Century* or the *North American Review*. Howells's nonfiction volumes were typically collections of literary essays and book columns that had already appeared in magazines. Sometimes he reissued these collections in later years in new and enlarged editions that he created by adding one or two new chapters to the book. These added chapters, of course, were themselves republished from earlier appearances in periodicals. The new material would be freshly typeset and plated; the remainder of the book would be reprinted from the original electrotypes.

The publication history of almost any one of Howells's major books is a study in recycling. For our purposes here, his collection *Literary Friends and Acquaintance* will demonstrate his practices as well as any. The book first appeared in a 288-page illustrated edition from Harper and Brothers in November 1900. Of the material in the volume, only Howells's introductory note was new. The chapters themselves were republished from *Harper's Monthly* or (in one instance) *Scribner's Magazine,* with some revision in each case. A limited edition of 150 copies was also printed in 1900 from these plates. By 1902, the collection was into its fifth trade printing. In 1910 Harper and Brothers reissued *Literary Friends* in an enlarged edition and the next year reissued it again as part of a proposed thirty-two-volume "Library Edition" of Howells's writings, a project that was never completed.[3] For these 1910 and 1911 reprints, the author supplied a new preface and added two more items, a sixteen-page chapter

2. Charvat, *The Profession of Authorship in America, 1800–1870,* pp. 61–67; idem, *Literary Publishing in America, 1790–1850* (Philadelphia: University of Pennsylvania Press, 1959), pp. 29–31; idem, *Emerson's American Lecture Engagements* (New York: New York Public Library, 1961).

3. Robert W. Walts, "William Dean Howells and His 'Library Edition,'" *Papers of the Bibliographical Society of America* 52 (4th Qtr., 1958): 283–94.

on Bret Harte, entitled "A Belated Guest," revised from its first appearance in Howells's column "Editor's Easy Chair" (*Harper's Monthly*, December 1903), and almost a hundred pages on Mark Twain that had already seen print twice before—once as "My Memories of Mark Twain," issued in installments in *Harper's Monthly* from July to September of 1910, and then immediately thereafter as "Part First" of *My Mark Twain: Reminiscences and Criticisms* (Harper and Brothers, 1910). The new sections dealing with Harte and Twain were freshly set up and plated for the Library Edition in a typeface and page design that matched the 1900 plates. Thus this last incarnation of *Literary Friends and Acquaintance* included material that had first been published as long as fifteen years before, and everything in the volume—with the exception of the preface and the piece on Harte—was seeing print for either the third or fourth time.

Novelist Frank Norris, whose work Howells admired, understood the techniques of recycling perfectly. In his essay "Fiction Writing as a Business," Norris imagined the various ways in which "a salable, readable, brisk bit of narrative" might be republished:

> Properly managed, this, under favourable conditions, might be its life history: First it is serialized either in the Sunday press or, less probably, in a weekly or monthly. Then it is made up into book form and sent over the course a second time. The original publisher sells sheets to a Toronto or Montreal house and a Canadian edition reaps a like harvest. It is not at all unlikely that a special cheap cloth edition may be bought and launched by some large retailer either of New York or Chicago. Then comes the paper edition—with small royalties, it is true, but based upon an enormous number of copies, for the usual paper edition is an affair of tens of thousands. Next the novel crosses the Atlantic and a small sale in England helps to swell the net returns, which again are added to—possibly—by the "colonial edition" which the English firm issues. Last of all comes the Tauchnitz edition, and with this (bar the improbable issuing of later special editions) the exploitation ceases. Eight separate times the same commodity has been sold, no one of the sales militating against the success of the other seven, the author getting his fair slice every time. Can any other trade, profession or art (excepting only the dramatist, which is, after all, a sister art) show the like? Even (speaking of the dramatist) there may be a ninth reincarnation of the same story and the creatures of the writer's pages stalk forth upon the boards in cloak and buskin.[4]

The American author who worked most assiduously to exploit the transatlantic publishing connections between Great Britain and the

4. In *The Responsibilities of the Novelist* (New York: Doubleday, Page, 1903), pp. 164–65.

United States was Henry James. His American citizenship and his English place of residence combined to protect him from most of the varieties of piracy that bedeviled American and British authors before 1891. James learned to play markets and publishers in New York and London against one another, and he worked cannily to build a readership for his writing both in his native land and in his adopted country. His market, he reckoned, would thereby be doubled. Other American fiction writers of the 1890s and early 1900s who took up residence in England—Stephen Crane, Harold Frederic, and Bret Harte, for example—followed James's example and sold to the English-language market on both sides of the Atlantic, ideally for magazine serialization as well as for book publication.[5]

Probably the most popular and commercially successful American novelist during the later years of James's career was George Barr McCutcheon, another master at recycling his work. McCutcheon wrote steadily from 1900 until his death in 1928, publishing during that period some forty-seven volumes, most of them light fiction. He kept a literary ledger in which he recorded virtually every penny he earned for his writing; that ledger survives today at the Beinecke Library. McCutcheon's ledger is especially valuable for its narrative portions: at the head of the entry for each book, he has written down the circumstances of composition, dates of typewriting, manner of serialization and book publication, and details of stage and screen adaptation. His ledger is a record of his entire professional career, and it reveals a great deal about the growing importance of subsidiary rights to the American author during the first quarter of the twentieth century.

McCutcheon, an Indiana native, attended Purdue University, where one of his fellow students was George Ade. Both worked as reporters after college; Ade quickly rose to fame in Chicago for his satirical columns and sketches, but McCutcheon's success did not come so rapidly. During the 1890s he worked for local papers in his home town of Lafayette and attempted without success to turn out playscripts in his spare time. In 1898, frustrated with his efforts at drama, he decided to try his hand at fiction. On his second attempt at a novel he produced his most popular narrative, a romance entitled *Graustark: The Story of a Love behind a Throne.* McCutcheon, however, was inexperienced at the business of authorship, and

5. Michael Anesko, *"Friction with the Market": Henry James and the Profession of Authorship* (New York: Oxford University Press, 1986), esp. pp. 33–51.

he made a major blunder in negotiating his contract for *Graustark*. Here, from his ledger, is his account of the mistake:

> This novel of 76000 words, was begun on Dec. 26, 1898, in the Columbia Apartment Building, Lafayette, Indiana, and was completed April 29, 1899. It was declined by Harper & Bros., and one or two other publishing houses, and was then completely rewritten. In the fall of 1899 it was submitted to H. S. Stone & Co., of Chicago, who accepted it, offering $500 cash for all rights or a royalty of 10%. Acting on the advice of George Ade, the author accepted the $500 in cash. The book was published on March 16, 1901, and was the Author's first published story, although "Nedra" was written before "Graustark". There were no illustrations in the original edition, which was small. The book did not begin to sell for several months, and then it went like a whirlwind.

In subsequent ledger paragraphs, McCutcheon details the success of *Graustark*. The novel went through numerous trade printings and into a reprint edition with Grosset and Dunlap; it was published successfully in England; it was translated into Danish, Norwegian, Italian, and Spanish; it was dramatized and presented throughout the country by as many as four road companies at once; and it was sold twice to the movies—once for a silent film in 1913 and later for a talkie remake starring Norma Talmadge in 1925. "The author," notes McCutcheon ruefully in the ledger, "never received a penny in the shape of royalties for book, play or motion pictures."

After *Graustark*, McCutcheon never made the mistake again of selling a literary work outright for a flat fee. His entry in the ledger for *Beverly of Graustark*, a 1904 sequel, is a good example of his later practice. He negotiated a straight 20 percent royalty with Dodd, Mead and Company and received a ten-thousand-dollar advance on publication day. He shared in the returns from British, Danish, and Norwegian editions and received royalties from a fifty-cent American reprint edition of 225,000 copies by Grosset and Dunlap. *Beverly* was dramatized by Robert Melville Baker; McCutcheon received escalating percentages of the theater gate and royalties from road and stock productions. Motion picture rights went initially to Biograph, but this sale resulted in litigation. The courts eventually decided in McCutcheon's favor, and in 1924 he was able to resell the movie rights to International for thirty thousand dollars, one-fourth of which went to Baker as dramatist. Second serial rights for the play were sold to the Hearst organization for an additional fifteen hundred dollars, also in

1924. McCutcheon had learned his lesson with *Graustark;* he never again allowed valuable subsidiary rights to slip through his fingers.[6]

According to Robert Frost, "Poetry has always been a beggar."[7] W. H. Auden wrote, "It is a sad fact about our culture that a poet can earn much more money writing or talking about his art than he can by practicing it."[8] Certainly both statements apply to the career of E. E. Cummings. In 1916, while still attending Harvard, Cummings decided to devote his life to poetry and painting. He made several attempts to hold down jobs in New York after he had finished his schooling, but he seems not to have been serious in these efforts. After he returned in 1918 from World War I, he never again held a true job. For support he trusted to luck and the generosity of others. As his college friend John Dos Passos put it, "He thought a poet should be fed by the ravens, and of course he was."[9] Cummings lived very frugally. He received money regularly from his parents until he was in his mid-fifties; these gifts, together with occasional grant and prize monies and a few dollars from the sale of a painting, allowed him to subsist. Essentially his writings brought him nothing. The publication of poetry in America has nearly always been a losing commercial proposition in this century; Cummings's avant-garde volumes were no exception. For most of his life he earned money from his verse only when he sold a poem to a magazine, and the outlets to which he sent his work—the *Dial* and *Vanity Fair,* for example—paid little.

In 1952 Cummings was offered the year-long Charles Eliot Norton Professorship at Harvard for fifteen thousand dollars. The only requirements were that he reside in Cambridge for the academic year and that he deliver a series of public lectures, which he could then publish with Harvard University Press if he chose to. The thought of giving these lectures

6. See James L. W. West III, "George Barr McCutcheon's Literary Ledger," *Yale University Library Gazette* 59 (April 1985): 155–61. Even in modern times, authors sometimes unwisely sell off subsidiary rights—usually before they realize what their full value might turn out to be. For example, in March 1964 Ian Fleming sold 51 percent of Gildrose Productions, his James Bond company, to Sir Jock Campbell for one hundred thousand pounds, most of which eventually went in death duties when Fleming's estate was settled. The sale took place shortly before the Bond craze caught on. See John Pearson, *The Life of Ian Fleming* (New York: McGraw-Hill, 1966), pp. 315–16.

7. From Frost's *Paris Review* interview, *Writers at Work,* ser. 2 (New York: Viking, 1963), p. 29.

8. From Auden's foreword to *The Dyer's Hand and Other Essays* (New York: Random House, 1962).

9. Quoted in the introduction to Richard S. Kennedy, *Dreams in the Mirror: A Biography of E. E. Cummings* (New York: Liveright, 1980), p. 5. Most of the biographical detail in this paragraph and the next is taken from Kennedy's volume.

terrified Cummings, but he needed the money and so undertook the professorship. His presentations, which he called "nonlectures," were enormously successful. He discovered that he had great talent as a reader of verse. Word of his ability spread, and he began to give readings at other campuses. Eventually he acquired an energetic lecture agent, Betty Kray (also Auden's agent), who arranged his appearances in geographically concentrated tours and persuaded him to standardize his honorarium. For a single reading Cummings received six or seven hundred dollars, depending on how far he had to travel. The great advantage of the procedure was that he was delivering verse orally that he had composed in much earlier periods. He was recycling his old creative efforts, drawing dividends from imaginative investments he had made long before. He also issued his works in collected and selected editions, and, like Longfellow, repeated the procedure with enlarged collected editions in later years. These volumes, published by Harcourt, Brace and Grove Press, sold well. Cummings made a good living in his late period by recycling his poetry, but it cost him many years of impecuniosity before he learned how to make his creative work pay. Campus readings proved to be the key for him; like Auden, he probably felt a backhanded affection for his college audiences:

> God bless the lot of them, although
> I don't remember which was which:
> God bless the U.S.A., so large,
> So friendly, and so rich.[10]

Recycling the Text

The major problem for American trade publishers, as we have seen in an earlier chapter, has always been distribution. Northeastern publishers were not able to establish a truly effective system of disseminating their product during the nineteenth century and did not show much aptitude for building up a national market for clothbound books until after World War II. In reaction, an alternative approach to book distribution—the mail-order book club—grew up during the 1920s and became spectacularly successful. Book-club publishers recognized that an existing mode of distribution, the U.S. postal service, could be adapted for literary

10. Auden, "On the Circuit," from *Selected Poems*, new ed., ed. Edward Mendelson (New York: Vintage, 1979), p. 250.

goods, especially after Rural Free Delivery was established. Harry Scherman and Maxwell Sackheim founded the Book-of-the-Month Club in 1926, and later that year Doubleday began the Literary Guild. Both clubs were successful, despite opposition from old-line publishers and booksellers, and they spawned many imitators. Scherman's simple insight was that post offices in America outnumbered traditional outlets for clothbound books ten to one. According to Scherman, publishers had always believed that it was impossible to sell single copies of books by mail at a profit "for the simple reason that the selling cost had to be charged against the single book." Scherman recognized the key: "The logic of it was that if the selling cost could be applied to or spread over a number of books, that problem could be solved."[11] The Book-of-the-Month Club, or BOMC as it is known, offered bonus books to new subscribers and advertised through mass-circulation magazines. During its early years, the club bought copies from trade publishers at a discount between 60 percent and 70 percent, a reduction made possible by the fact that the trade publisher could simply extend the print run and lower the cost per copy of the entire impression. Later, book clubs began to lease original or duplicate plates on a royalty basis (with a minimum guarantee of royalty) and to print their own copies.[12] This practice allowed trade publishers and book clubs to cover each other if a book got "hot"—something that happened, for example, with Sinclair Lewis's *Cass Timberlane*.[13] More recently, clubs have moved away from royalty payments toward flat-fee purchase of book-club rights. The advantages to the book club are that it no longer has to keep careful records of sales and can regulate its own printing runs more efficiently. The advantage to the author and the original publisher is that they receive their money before publication and can immediately spend it or put it to work. The book club assumes the entire risk of selling the edition and is encouraged, when it pays out the flat fee in advance, to advertise the book strongly enough to recoup its investment.

In 1927, its first full year of operation, BOMC had net sales of $1,641,210 and net earnings of $152,136 before taxes. The Great Depression began

11. From Scherman's section of the BOMC Oral History, Columbia University, New York, pp. 36–37 of the transcript.

12. Ibid., p. 50.

13. *Cass Timberlane* production folder, Box 214, Random House Papers, Columbia University, New York. The first trade printing was for ninety-two thousand copies, but Random House still had to borrow additional copies from BOMC. The borrowing went in the opposite direction for William Faulkner's *The Reivers* (1962) and William Styron's *The Confessions of Nat Turner* (1967); collectors often find trade sheets for both books in BOMC casings and jackets.

two years later, but book clubs, and publishers generally, weathered it quite well. As Scherman recognized, "Book buying is undoubtedly less dependent on the economic level of the public than on its reading level." By 1945, net sales for BOMC had reached $13,678,225 and net earnings $2,818,816. The gross margin of profit in that year was an astonishing 75 percent as against 34 percent for traditional bookstores.[14] Book clubs had discovered a way to reach what BOMC historian Charles Lee called "the hidden public." Established trade publishers, however, feared the rise of book clubs and fought them vigorously until the mid-1950s. Traditional publishers maintained that book-club marketing was simply another form of price-cutting and loss-leadering. Bookstore operators in particular feared that the clubs, which sold book-club editions at a discount, would put them out of business. Advocates of the book clubs insisted that they reached a different public from the one served by bookshops. These persons argued that massive book-club advertising campaigns in magazines and newsletters actually stimulated sales of trade editions. Traditional publishers were unpersuaded; Maxwell Perkins, for example, continued to feel that book clubs intensified the "racket" element in publishing.[15] By the 1950s, however, the clubs had become so successful that publishers were forced to learn to coexist with them, and the clubs became a significant way by which literary work could be recycled in printed form.

Several twentieth-century American authors were helped greatly by the book clubs. F. Scott Fitzgerald was not: he turned down the only offer he ever received—Literary Guild wanted *Tender Is the Night* as an alternate selection in 1934—because he feared that club circulation would injure trade sales. But Ernest Hemingway, John Steinbeck, and James Gould Cozzens reached huge audiences through the clubs. Steinbeck in particular was well served by BOMC. Six of his books—*Of Mice and Men, The Moon Is Down, The Red Pony, The Wayward Bus, Sweet Thursday,* and *The Short Reign of Pippin IV*—were featured selections or alternates for BOMC from 1937 to 1957; almost surely he reached his largest audiences through the clubs.[16]

14. Scherman, "The Book-of-the-Month Club, Inc." (speech to investors, ca. 1945), Harry Scherman Collection, Columbia University, New York.

15. Perkins to Conrad Aiken, 11 December 1939, Scribner Archive, Princeton University, Princeton, N.J.

16. Year-by-year lists of BOMC selections, alternates, and dividends, 1926–57, are included in Charles Lee, *The Hidden Public: The Story of the Book-of-the-Month Club* (Garden City, N.Y.: Doubleday, 1958), pp. 161–94.

Omnibus volumes, sold through book clubs, could also build readership for an author's other writings. Eugene O'Neill's collection *Nine Plays,* for example, had sold some 97,315 copies through BOMC by 1937, giving O'Neill's name and work enormous exposure. Bennett Cerf explained to O'Neill, who was worried about his reduced royalty on book-club sales, that regular bookstores could never have sold so many copies. These traditional outlets had such limited shelf space that they could order only one or two copies at a time.[17] In addition to wide exposure, selection of a book as a featured choice by one of the major book clubs could bring a major jump in an author's income. Stephen Vincent Benét's literary earnings in 1927 were a mere $2,386.79. In 1928, when *John Brown's Body* was chosen as the August selection of BOMC, his income rose to $13,197.25.[18]

As long as books were submitted to club juries in finished form, printed and bound, the clubs could have no influence on the text of a book. The jury either took a book or turned it down. During the late 1930s, however, books began to be submitted in galley proof so that the huge magazine and mail-order advertising campaigns would coincide with trade publication. Now there was an opportunity for prepublication influence from book-club juries. In 1942, BOMC juror Henry Seidel Canby required Robert Trumbull to make cuts in *The Raft* before the club would take the novel for distribution.[19] Ross Lockridge, Jr.'s, novel *Raintree County* was bowdlerized before publication in this same way; BOMC wanted the book as its January 1948 selection but only if the author would change several passages its jury found offensive. Lockridge made the alterations and reaped a large financial reward.[20] Similar cases have likely occurred over the years, but none has yet come to light. Most

17. Cerf to O'Neill, 14 September 1937, Random House Papers.

18. Benét's tax records from Brandt and Brandt, Benét Collection, Beinecke Library, Yale University, New Haven, Conn.

19. Henry Holt Co. to BOMC, 19 August 1942, Holt Collection, Princeton University, Princeton, N.J. For this book, BOMC entered into a trial arrangement with King Features, which agreed to syndicate daily newspaper "visualizations" of this BOMC selection in order to encourage subscriptions. King Features paid the artist, then divided remaining revenues from the newspapers evenly with BOMC. King expected to gross approximately five thousand dollars per book.

20. Lee, *The Hidden Public,* pp. 122–23. BOMC also attempted to have George Orwell alter *1984.* According to Orwell, the club wished him to cut between a fifth and a quarter of the book and then tack on the last chapter to the "abbreviated trunk." Orwell refused; BOMC capitulated and published the book uncut. See *The Collected Essays, Journalism and Letters of George Orwell,* vol. 4, ed. Sonia Orwell and Ian Angus (Harmondsworth, Eng.: Penguin, 1970), pp. 544–45.

book clubs are closemouthed about their selection processes and manufacturing procedures; historians of the twentieth-century book trade and bibliographers of modern authors have usually had no luck trying to pry information from them.

Another popular way of recycling the text of a literary work was for the publisher to lease the original plates to a cheap reprint series. Many inexpensive reprint operations were in business in America before World War II: Grosset and Dunlap, A. L. Burt, Blue Ribbon Books, the Dollar Book Club, the Modern Library, and several others. All survived by offering clothbound reprints at low prices, often a dollar or less. The books were sold through nontraditional outlets such as department stores and newsstands. Prices were low because the books, though clothbound, were manufactured in long print runs with cheap materials and with a minimum of overhead. The author accepted reduced royalties. This was a good way to keep a book available in hardback; famous novels like *Sister Carrie* and *The Sun Also Rises* were carried by Grosset and Dunlap, for example, and *This Side of Paradise* was reprinted for a time by A. L. Burt. But the timing of a cheap reprint was crucial, because the inexpensive books could potentially kill off trade sales. H. L. Mencken was convinced that the Blue Ribbon Books reprinting of *Treatise on the Gods* had ruined the long-term trade sale of the Knopf edition.[21] And B. W. Huebsch almost surely damaged Sherwood Anderson's sales and reputation by allowing Anderson's best books to go into cheap reprint editions too early. After their initial trade runs slowed down, Huebsch quickly placed *Winesburg, Ohio* and *Poor White* into the Modern Library; *Many Marriages* went to Grosset and Dunlap, *Horses and Men* to Cape and Smith's "Travellers' Library," and *A Story Teller's Story* to Garden City Publishing Company's "Star Dollar Series." Huebsch got a small continuing royalty for these reprint sales, and he no longer had to bother about promoting, selling, and storing the back stock—activities he was not much interested in. The results for Anderson were unfortunate. His books were nearly all out of print by the mid-1930s, and toward the end of his life his backlist royalties dwindled to almost nothing. Anderson was bitter, with good reason. His career never recovered from this early mismanagement; in fact, his reputation today would probably be higher

21. Mary Miller Vass and James L. W. West III, "The Composition and Revision of Mencken's *Treatise on the Gods*," *Papers of the Bibliographical Society of America* 77 (4th Qtr., 1983): 455.

had he allied himself with a stronger, more savvy publisher. In this case, attempts to recycle works of literature too early in the game were harmful to an important author.[22]

The notion of serializing a novel in the newspaper *after* its publication in book form is unheard of today. In the 1920s, however, it was common practice, simply one more way of recycling the text of a literary work. Most large-circulation newspapers carried what were known as "second serials" on the back pages of each issue. Popular novels and short stories were served up piecemeal to readers in this fashion. Often a syndicate would handle second serial rights for a novel or story and would place it in many of the newspapers in its chain. The money paid for second serial rights was small—a full-length novel brought from $150 to $250 per newspaper—but the exposure was enormous. F. Scott Fitzgerald's first and second novels were serialized after book publication in the *Washington Herald,* the *Chicago Herald and Examiner,* the *New York Daily News,* and the *Atlanta Georgian.* Through these papers his fiction was made available to approximately a million and a half readers. There was a drawback, however: all of these newspapers treated his texts irresponsibly, cutting and censoring them for serial presentation. Fitzgerald's novels were available to some of their largest audiences in butchered and botched form.[23]

One of the most important ways of recycling the text of a literary work was the paperback, or the "drugstore edition," to use Flannery O'Connor's term. Many people believe that paperback publication did not exist before 1935—that the technology for printing and binding paper-covered books had not been developed before that time. Actually it had been possible to produce paperbacks almost from the earliest years of the printing industry, and paperbacks had been marketed in America periodically since the middle of the nineteenth century. The earliest paperback publishers in this country operated from about 1840 until 1845; they were pirates and price-cutters, like Park Benjamin and Rufus W. Griswold, who specialized in reprinting popular British writings in both newspaper and book format. These early speculators created havoc in the book trade and eventually eliminated one another. The second group of paperback manufacturers was similar. Such men as Erastus Beadle, George P. Munro, Or-

---

22. Hilbert H. Campbell, "Sherwood Anderson and the Viking Press, 1925–1941," *Resources for American Literary Study* 10 (Autumn 1980): 167–72.

23. James L. W. West III, "The Second Serials of *This Side of Paradise* and *The Beautiful and Damned,*" *Papers of the Bibliographical Society of America* 73 (1st Qtr., 1979): 63–74. Also see H. H. McClure, "The Syndicate Racket," *American Spectator,* February 1933, pp. 2, 4.

mond Smith, John W. Lovell, and Frank Leslie published huge "libraries" of cheap fiction designed to undercut the market for traditional editions. These publishers managed to survive from about 1880 until 1893 and again ruined themselves by overproduction. They were hastened to their demise by the first international copyright law in 1891, which ended the worst forms of transatlantic piracy, and by a depression in 1893. Neither group of early paperbound publishers was of much value to the serious American author. These publishers were in business for quick profits, and they specialized in pirating the work of British authors. Most of the original writings by native authors that they published were thrillers and dime novels.

By the time the third American experiment in paperback publishing came along in the late 1930s conditions had changed. Old-line American publishers were leery of paperbacks; some of them were old enough to remember the difficulties of the 1880s and 1890s and were not eager to repeat them. The major New York trade houses therefore watched, very carefully, the progress of Pocket Books, the first modern American paperback firm, established in 1939. When Ian Ballantine, who had made his start with Penguin in England, founded Bantam Books as a competitor for Pocket Books in 1945, the major trade publishers were careful to buy into the experiment. They did so through their combined ownership of Grosset and Dunlap, which they had bought as a group the previous year to prevent its falling into the hands of department-store magnate Marshall Field. Grosset and Dunlap owned 50 percent of Bantam; Curtis Publishing Company in Philadelphia owned the other half. Eventually Curtis sold out, and Bantam came entirely under the ownership of Grosset and Dunlap. Through this connection, trade publishers helped keep authors' royalties on paperbacks quite low for a number of years— 4 percent on sales up to 150,000, 6 percent thereafter. The major trade publishers thus helped control the direction of paperback publishing in this country during the early 1940s.[24]

During World War II, John Farrar, W. W. Norton, Malcolm Johnson, and other publishers founded the Council on Books in Wartime in order to provide cheap reading matter for servicemen. After settling on a revolutionary format—a small paperback approximately $5\frac{1}{2}$ by 4 inches, se-

24. Charles A. Madison, "The Paperback Explosion," *Book Publishing in America* (New York: McGraw-Hill, 1966), pp. 547–56; *At Random: The Reminiscences of Bennett Cerf* (New York: Random House, 1977), p. 198.

cured by a staple through the spine—the council began to issue Armed Services Editions and, later, Overseas Editions in English. By the end of the war, some 123.5 million copies of 1,324 different books had been issued—a great stimulus for the growth of paperback publishing. Armed Services Editions showed publishers that there was a large audience for paperbacks, and after the war the industry boomed. Today the major paperback houses are quite powerful in the literary marketplace. The money offered for best-seller paperback rights is quite large. Thirty years ago, most books brought from fifteen hundred to ten thousand dollars; a figure of fifteen thousand dollars was probably the upper limit. Today, competitive bidding and shopping-center distribution have forced prices for paperback rights much higher, and it is not uncommon for a book to fetch more than a million dollars.

Adapting the Text

By the 1920s, two important new methods for recycling literary work had become firmly established—dramatic adaptations and movie versions. One of the American authors who benefited handsomely from these developments during the twenties was F. Scott Fitzgerald. His first two novels, *This Side of Paradise* and *The Beautiful and Damned,* were strong sellers but not true best-sellers. Each book sold about fifty thousand copies. *The Great Gatsby* (1925), perhaps Fitzgerald's finest novel, barely made expenses and earned just enough to balance off the advances he had drawn from his publisher. As we shall see, however, Harold Ober's astuteness as literary agent enabled Fitzgerald to exploit the dramatic and movie rights to *Gatsby* in such a way that the novel generated almost twenty thousand dollars of extra income the year after it appeared in print.

The economics of the American stage were entirely different in 1925 from what they are in the 1980s. There were at that time some seventy-five theater buildings in New York City, and there were approximately 250 new productions mounted on Broadway annually. About half were musicals or revues, the other half spoken drama. It cost a mere ten thousand to forty thousand dollars to mount a spoken drama and between forty thousand and seventy-five thousand dollars to put on a musical. A good run for a show was three months; six weeks was usually enough to break even.[25] Productions were relatively modest in scope and staging, and the rate of failure was high. Broadway producers like the Frohman brothers and David Belasco were constantly on the lookout for fresh material, and many of the best-selling books of the day were dramatized and enjoyed good stage runs. The authors of these books benefited in several ways. They received flat fees for drama rights, or they were paid percentages of the box office if the show had a long run. When the drama went on tour, more money was forthcoming. The exposure of an author's name and of the book's title was excellent for the author's career and for the sale of other writings by the author. Sometimes there was even a backwash effect: a successful play could reactivate sales of a novel and stimulate readers to buy it after they had seen it dramatized.

Occasionally the book would be adapted for the stage by its author, but that did not happen with *Gatsby*. Fitzgerald took no active part in its dramatization or staging; the story was adapted by Owen Davis, one of the most successful stage writers of the twenties, and was produced by William A. Brady. Ober negotiated a good contract. Fitzgerald received escalating percentages of the gate: 40 percent of 5 percent of the first five thousand dollars, 40 percent of 7.5 percent of the next two thousand dollars, and 40 percent of 10 percent of all receipts after that. *Gatsby* opened in early February 1926, starring Ernest Truax in the title role, and ran for four months. Some weeks it grossed more than fifteen thousand dollars. Fitzgerald's share was six hundred dollars, and he did not have to lift a finger to collect it.[26]

Stimulated by the success of *Gatsby* on the stage, the Hollywood production firm Famous Players purchased rights to the book for a movie version. Film rights were a relatively new thing in the 1920s; they often went for very little, but they would eventually prove to be a major source of income for American writers. The economic structure of the film industry was also quite different then from what it is in the 1980s. The major studios had large permanent staffs and kept directors, technicians, and other support workers on salary. Each studio had a number of stars

25. Alfred L. Bernheim, *The Business of the Theatre: An Economic History of the American Theatre, 1750–1932* (New York: Benjamin Blom, Inc., 1964), originally published in installments in *Equity Magazine,* July 1930–February 1932.

26. *As Ever, Scott Fitz—Letters between F. Scott Fitzgerald and His Literary Agent Harold Ober, 1919–1940,* ed. Matthew J. Bruccoli and Jennifer McCabe Atkinson (Philadelphia: Lippincott, 1972), p. 79n.

under contract. These people could not be left idle. A great many more feature films were produced then than now, and theater runs were much shorter. Movie moguls, like drama producers, were constantly in search of fresh material, and one dependable source was recently published novels. Many studios kept a staff of readers on hand to go through current novels and manuscripts to assess their movie potential. In fact, that was Lillian Hellman's first job in Hollywood, at Metro-Goldwyn-Mayer, for fifty dollars a week.[27]

Famous Players turned *Gatsby* into a successful film. The novel was adapted for the screen by Elizabeth Mechan, and again the production starred Ernest Truax. Sound tracks had not yet been added to the movies, so this first screen version of *Gatsby* was a silent film. That fact is important because a few years later, when the talkies arrived, a number of authors were able to sell the screen rights to their popular novels a second time. The courts ruled that the original sales had included silent-film rights only. Sound rights were still the author's property, and this interpretation allowed many writers to collect money twice from Hollywood. Fitzgerald did not live to do so, but his heirs sold the sound rights to *Gatsby* to Paramount in the 1940s, and the novel was made into a gangster movie starring Alan Ladd, Macdonald Carey, and Shelley Winters.

The original 1926 sale of *Gatsby* to Hollywood seems also to have called Fitzgerald's name to the attention of John Considine of United Artists, and in 1927 Fitzgerald was hired to produce a movie idea or "treatment" for Constance Talmadge, then under contract with United. Fitzgerald produced a bit of flapper foolishness called "Lipstick" about a girl who gets hold of a magic lipstick that makes her irresistibly kissable. United never shot the film, but Fitzgerald got thirty-five hundred dollars and a trip to Hollywood—indirect benefits, it would seem, of the film version of *Gatsby*.[28]

Early contracts for motion picture rights were similar to early agreements for drama rights. Studios usually paid publishers and authors a flat fee plus a percentage of weekly box-office receipts. Among the business papers of authors whose work was popular before 1925, one often finds statements of weekly attendance at movie theaters throughout the

27. Lillian Hellman, *An Unfinished Woman—A Memoir* (Boston: Little, Brown, 1969), p. 57.
28. Matthew J. Bruccoli, *Some Sort of Epic Grandeur: The Life of F. Scott Fitzgerald* (New York: Harcourt Brace Jovanovich, 1981), p. 259. "Lipstick" was published in the 1978 *Fitzgerald/Hemingway Annual*.

country. An author's share of ticket-sale money was computed from those statements. This kind of record-keeping, however, proved to be so troublesome and fostered so many charges of dishonesty that movie studios came to prefer flat-fee arrangements.

In the early years of Hollywood, studios acquired movie rights to many popular literary works in perpetuity, and in the 1940s and 1950s they discovered that they could turn out remakes of earlier popular movies without having to pay additional money to authors. Edna Ferber saw her 1924 best-seller *So Big* made into a second movie version in 1950 and wrote unhappily to her former agent, "As contracts signed with motion picture people in the far-off days of the first publication of SO BIG were sort of world-without-end affairs, the refilming of this novel will yield me exactly nothing."[29] Authors and agents learned to insist on time-lease contracts for movie rights. Studios would pay a fee for movie rights over a stated period of time—usually five to ten years—after which authors were free to sell the rights again.

Movie studios were primarily interested in lightweight fiction. Goldwyn Producing Corporation, a forerunner of Metro-Goldwyn-Mayer, turned down Stephen Vincent Benét's bildungsroman *The Beginning of Wisdom*, for example, because the novel was too highbrow. In declining the book, Goldwyn instructed Henry Holt to send, in the future, only "sure-fire stuff . . . melodrama with a punch."[30] Some studios did buy rights to serious fiction, however, and publishers learned to pursue such sales. Galleys of virtually every book published by Liveright during the late 1920s were sent to MGM, Fox, RKO, Paramount, Warner Brothers, and other studios. Most of the time such angling came to nothing, but it took only one sale to make the entire procedure worthwhile.[31] Movie people, for their part, learned that large book sales could attract big audiences to theaters. As a result, clauses in movie-rights contracts during the late 1940s began to guarantee bonuses to authors if their books sold over specified numbers of copies. Such clauses were in effect incentives to publishers (who would share the bonuses) to push sales of these books as hard as possible and, in that way, prepare the public for the upcoming

29. Ferber to Flora May Holly, 9 August 1950, Holly Collection, Manuscripts Division, New York Public Library.

30. Goldwyn Producing Corp. to Henry Holt, undated, Box 42, Holt Collection.

31. The correspondence between Liveright and these various Hollywood studios is in the Liveright Collection, Special Collections, Van Pelt Library, University of Pennsylvania, Philadelphia, Pa.

movies. These incentive clauses are found in almost all contracts for movie rights in the 1970s and 1980s. The agreement for William Styron's *Sophie's Choice,* for example, specifies that the producer will pay fifty cents to Styron and Random House for every clothbound copy sold over twenty thousand.[32]

During the 1940s, contracts for movie rights became exceedingly complicated. The essential purpose of such documents was to differentiate between (1) a license to base a film on a literary work and (2) outright sale of motion picture rights to that work. Under the latter arrangement, the author sold off film rights in perpetuity; under a licensing arrangement, the author parted with them only for a specified period of time, after which those rights either reverted back or could be extended by a series of options built into the contract. Additional matters for negotiation included whether the movie production unit could itself sell, license, or transfer to other parties certain additional rights inherent in the movie (songs, music, dialogue on the sound track, costumes, sets, posters—also rights to abridgment for advertising purposes, to radio broadcast of parts of the sound track, and to television presentation). At issue were two other matters: whether failure to carry through filming to completion and subsequent distribution effectively shelved the property for the duration of the license and whether compensation would be in the form of flat payment, stock in the production company, percentage of net, percentage of gross, or some combination of these. Also important were ownership of copyright to the film (always initially by the production company but sometimes transferred in part to the author after the final right to exhibit had expired) and the author's billing on posters and credits for the film. The crucial point for an author and an agent to understand was that the author created all of these rights in the act of composing a story or play. It was then the author's decision whether to sell these rights, lease them, or perhaps retain them for future exploitation after the author's reputation had grown.

Drama rights could be as lucrative as movie rights. As early as the 1890s, Daniel Frohman was securing options on drama rights to literary material, usually for six-month periods. He frequently traveled to England, just as American trade publishers did, in order to secure U.S. drama

---

32. Such a clause is in the contract for Marquand's *B. F.'s Daughter,* for example (T. J. Robinson of MGM to Carl Brandt, 12 January 1948, Marquand Collection, Yale University, New Haven, Conn.). Information about *Sophie's Choice* is from Styron to West, 19 March 1983.

rights to promising British novels. Frohman scored a major commercial coup in America with his stage production of Anthony Hope Hawkins's *The Prisoner of Zenda* (1894), which grossed more than ten thousand dollars per week at the height of its long run in New York during 1894 and 1895. Frohman produced dramatic versions of some serious novels as well—he put Thomas Hardy's *Tess of the D'Urbervilles* on the American stage with moderate success, for example—but much of what he dealt with was popular fare. He declined the drama rights to one Macmillan novel, one notes, because there was "not enough of a central love story to make an effective play."[33]

Frohman's arrangements with publishing houses were similar to the contracts between those publishers and their authors. For Agnes Castle and Egerton Castle's *The Pride of Jennico,* published by Macmillan in 1898, Frohman agreed to pay 5 percent of his weekly gate receipts up to five thousand dollars, 10 percent of the next two thousand dollars, and 15 percent thereafter. These monies were to be divided equally between Macmillan and the author of the stage adaptation; Macmillan then split its share with the Castles. Frohman saw early in the game that a successful production could stimulate sales of a book: "Would it be a good idea, for the sale of 'The Pride of Jennico', to push the book in the cities wherein the play is to appear?" he wrote George Brett at Macmillan. "Do you publish cheap, or paper editions, as was done in the case of 'The Prisoner of Zenda'?"[34]

Some twentieth-century American novelists have tried their own hands at drama, a genre that has great earning potential if the author's contract with the producer has been properly negotiated. Fitzgerald believed that his three-act play *The Vegetable* (1922) would be a financial success, and at his urging agent Harold Ober took care to set up the business end properly. Fitzgerald's contract with producer Sam H. Harris gave him a five-hundred-dollar advance on his share of gross weekly box-office receipts; he would get 5 percent of the first five thousand dollars, 7.5 percent of the next twenty-five hundred dollars, and 10 percent thereafter. Fitzgerald also kept all book, serial, magazine, newspaper, and musical rights. Harris, for his part, received U.S. and Canadian production rights and held an option on English, British Isles, and Empire rights. In an important clause frequently found in drama contracts after 1920, Harris and Fitzgerald

33. Frohman to George Brett, 10 November 1899, Macmillan Collection, Manuscripts Division, New York Public Library.
34. Frohman to Brett, 16 September 1898 and 3 February 1900, Macmillan Collection.

would divide world moving picture rights equally if the stage production reached fifty performances during the first year after its premiere. (The assumption was that a successful theater run would be largely responsible for drawing an offer from Hollywood; the producer therefore ought to share in the movie money.) If the play ran for more than fifty performances, Harris was also to receive a half-interest in stock, amateur, and repertoire receipts, with Fitzgerald retaining the other 50 percent. If *The Vegetable* had been a success, both Fitzgerald and Harris would have profited handsomely from these various residuals, but to Fitzgerald's great disappointment the play flopped in Atlantic City and was never staged in New York.

Theodore Dreiser's 1926 arrangement with Horace Liveright for drama rights to *An American Tragedy* was similar to Fitzgerald's contract with Harris. The chief difference was that Dreiser had to share his percentages with Patrick Kearny, who had adapted the massive novel for the stage. Dreiser and Kearny received a fifteen hundred dollar advance; their share of the gate was 5 percent of the first four thousand dollars, 7.5 percent of the next three thousand dollars, and 10 percent thereafter. Dreiser and Kearny, however, were careful to retain a controlling 55 percent of all subsidiary rights, including amateur, stock, little theater, chatauqua, repertoire, and tent-show productions. Fitzgerald and Harris had split those residuals equally, making for potential difficulty had they disagreed on their disposal. In such cases, according to the *Vegetable* contract, one party would have had to buy out the other.[35]

A dramatist like Eugene O'Neill looked at publication of his plays in the same way that a novelist like Dreiser looked at adaptation of his fiction for the stage—as a lucrative way of recycling his work in another medium. O'Neill's plays sold widely in printed form, and when he left Liveright in 1933 he took pains to negotiate, through his agent Richard J. Madden, an advantageous new three-year contract with Random House for publication of his drama scripts. O'Neill received a ten-thousand-dollar advance against two new plays and a straight royalty of 20 percent on each copy sold.[36] Random House promised to publish a new series of editions of O'Neill's plays but asked O'Neill not to mention these new

35. Fitzgerald's contract with Harris for *The Vegetable* and the contract between Dreiser/Kearny and Liveright for *An American Tragedy* are both in the files of the American Play Co., Berg Collection, New York Public Library.
36. A preliminary annotated draft and a final file copy of O'Neill's first contract with Random House are in the O'Neill files, Random House Papers.

editions for the time being, because Random House wanted to get rid of the old stock it had inherited from Liveright. O'Neill was especially conscious of the need to coordinate the publication of his plays with their New York premieres. Advertising of the published versions had to begin well before the premieres, and copies of the plays had to be ready for sale when the productions hit the boards. For O'Neill this was sometimes a problem, for he often revised his plays in proof right up until press time in order to incorporate alterations made in rehearsals. Consequently, the standard clause in a publisher's contract requiring the author to pay for proof alterations that exceed 10 percent of the typesetting charges caused difficulties for O'Neill. He had Random House strike this clause from a preliminary version of the new contract and explained his reasons in a letter to Cerf:

> If publication simultaneous with production is desired, with galleys set up by the time rehearsals start, then I must be allowed a free hand to incorporate in the galleys any changes or cuts that rehearsals reveal as valuable to the play. I know this clause is part of the usual contract and I agree that it is fair as regards novels, etc., but in the case of a play when publication at the same time as production is an asset to the publisher, it seems to me a mistake—for I can't, in justice to my work, call a script final until rehearsals are well along.[37]

Publishers learned to exploit the production/publication tie-in by having copies of the published play on sale in the lobby of the theater in which the production was being presented. For New York productions this was relatively easy, but when a company went on the road it was difficult to ensure that the books would be shipped properly and would arrive on the right day. By the time O'Neill's *Ah, Wilderness* went on tour in the mid-1930s Random House had learned to secure the traveling schedule ahead of time and to coordinate efforts with the Theatre Guild.

Other ancillary income came to O'Neill from cheap pamphlet editions of his plays printed for the Dramatists Play Service by Random House and sold to that organization at a 47 percent discount. These pamphlet editions, sent out to amateur groups for local productions, were a good way for the publisher to dispose of remaindered stock.[38] Samuel French, another publisher of drama scripts, either purchased old stock or leased plates from the original publisher of a play in order to manufacture its own editions. French paid five cents per copy on copies sold; the pub-

37. O'Neill to Cerf, 4 June 1933, Random House Papers.
38. Box 97A, Random House Papers.

lisher usually split that money equally with the playwright. The returns were small—most of the Samuel French editions numbered between five hundred and one thousand copies—but the exposure of the dramatist's name and work through amateur groups was wide.[39]

Radio provided another medium for which literature could be adapted. Popular short stories from mass-circulation magazines were frequently turned into radio scripts that were then broadcast nationwide. (For a short time during the 1930s, New York trade publishers began to speak of radio as a serious threat to the book business, much as they blame television today for the decline in reading.) Most of the published writing that was presented on the radio was popular-level entertainment; nearly all of the detective stories of Robert W. Chambers, for example, were turned into radio scripts soon after publication. But some serious literature also was adapted for radio. Anderson's "I'm a Fool" and Fitzgerald's "The Diamond as Big as the Ritz," for example, were presented over the airwaves. Of important American writers, Dashiell Hammett benefited most from radio adaptation of his work. Several of his short stories were made into radio scripts, and Hammett himself turned out a few original plots for radio broadcast. Later in his career, after the great success of *The Thin Man* in 1934, he simply leased out the radio rights to his work for three different radio serials—"The Adventures of the Thin Man," "The Fat Man" (based on Hammett's Continental Op), and "The Adventures of Sam Spade." Other writers devised the story lines and churned out the dialogue; Hammett sat back and collected some thirteen hundred dollars per week in royalties. This radio money was almost his sole income from 1946 until 1951. In that year his radio royalties were attached by the Internal Revenue Service for Hammett's failure to pay back taxes. He was ruined financially and was a pauper for the rest of his life.[40]

Willard Motley's *Knock on Any Door* is an example of a successful novel that was adapted in several ways for later publication and re-presentation. The novel, a sociologically oriented study of the making of a criminal, was published initially by Appleton-Century in May 1947 and almost immediately began to sell in large numbers. During the months that followed, while the novel was on the *New York Times* best-seller list, Motley received payments for its republication as a Fiction Book Club selection ($18,000), for a "picture dramatization" in *Look* magazine ($1,500), for a

39. Box 38, Holt Collection.

40. Richard Layman, *Shadow Man: The Life of Dashiell Hammett* (New York: Harcourt Brace Jovanovich, 1981), p. 203.

condensation in *Omnibook* ($1,750), and for a condensed newspaper serial for King Features ($750 plus half of the additional profits). *Knock on Any Door* also became a Signet Double Volume for a $25,000 advance plus later royalties and a Columbia Pictures film, starring Humphrey Bogart, for a price of more than $65,000. After the release of the film, the magazine *Movie Story* reversed the direction of things and published a sixty-two-hundred-word condensation of the movie. Motley was not eager to claim parentage of these various incarnations of his novel (his response to the movie: "It ain't my kid! It's a bastard!"), but he must have been happy about the monetary returns.[41]

Contracts

A new consciousness of the importance of subsidiary rights is reflected in authors' contracts with their publishers after about 1910. Gertrude Atherton could still be very casual in negotiating a 1901 agreement with George Brett at Macmillan: "There is no hurry about the contract," she wrote him regarding an agreement for a proposed collection of her short stories. "There will not be much money in them, and you can have them for what you choose."[42] Edna Ferber, seventeen years later, was not nearly so offhand with Brett about contractual terms. For a collection of her stories (the first of her books to be published by Macmillan), Brett had sent Ferber a simple royalty contract that made no mention of subsidiary rights. Ferber wrote back:

> The royalty terms of the contract sent me are fair and even generous. But surely, Mr. Brett, you know I could not sign a contract that does not even touch on:
>   Dramatic Rights
>   Moving Picture Rights
>   Second Serial Rights
>   Cheap Edition Royalties or Rights.
> The first three have always been granted outright, and a definite sum agreed on the last.

Brett, one of the most conservative publishers of his time, still believed that book publishers had no business dealing with such residuals. He responded to Ferber:

---

41. Craig S. Abbott, "Versions of a Best-Seller: Motley's *Knock on Any Door,*" *Papers of the Bibliographical Society of America* 81 (June 1987): 175–85.
42. Atherton to Brett, 4 December [1901], Macmillan Collection.

> We are advised by counsel that neither dramatic nor motion picture rights are included in our standard form of contract and that this form of contract, which is the one submitted to you, covers the publishing rights in book form only; consequently we never put into our contracts any mention of the dramatic or motion picture rights, knowing well that we have no claim on such rights and no interest in them.[43]

Brett's attitude did not endear him to literary agents. In 1920 he sold, at one crack, the cinema rights to thirty-eight of the recently deceased F. Marion Crawford's novels to Italian film producer Amerigo Serrano. A. P. Watt, the London agent who handled Crawford's English rights, learned of the arrangement and exploded. Brett had sold the rights in perpetuity for 3.5 percent of net profits, which, according to Watt, could be manipulated by the movie people. He maintained that the rights should have been released only for a period of five years and that the percentage should have been calculated on gross receipts, which could not be so easily fiddled with. Brett's reply was testy: clearly he regarded film rights as a nuisance and simply wanted them off his hands.[44]

The ways in which a literary work could be made to yield income multiplied so rapidly after 1920, however, that publishers like Brett had to learn to be more attentive. According to editor Maxwell Perkins, the mystery writer Arthur Train began to think about film possibilities while he was still planning his novels. "He calls conferences of his magazine editor, his movie producer, and of me as representing his publisher," wrote Perkins to Charles Scribner, Jr., in February 1925. "There his manuscript is discussed scene by scene. It's a strange way to write a book."[45] By the late 1920s, standard publishers' contracts had begun to mention all kinds of subsidiary possibilities—book clubs, magazine serials, second serials, abridgments, translations, syndications, and paperback rights in addition to drama, radio, and movie rights. There were even popular songs based on Fitzgerald's *This Side of Paradise*, Hemingway's *A Farewell to Arms*, and Wolfe's *Of Time and the River*.[46] The standard arrangement

---

43. Ferber to Brett, 8 January 1918; and Brett to Ferber, 9 January 1918, Macmillan Collection.

44. Crawford files, Macmillan Collection, esp. Watt to F. W. Holme, 16 June 1920, and Brett to Holme, 22 July 1920.

45. Perkins to Charles Scribner, Jr., 24 February 1925, Sherwood Anderson files, Scribner Archive.

46. Fitzgerald mentions the song based on *This Side of Paradise* in his literary ledger. See *F. Scott Fitzgerald's Ledger: A Facsimile*, ed. Matthew J. Bruccoli (Washington, D.C.: NCR/Microcard, 1972), p. 3. The song was copyrighted by Paul Stanton following the deposit of one copy at the Library of Congress on 28 August 1920. Sheet music of the 1933 song

was for receipts from such recyclings to be split fifty-fifty between publisher and author.

During the first half of the twentieth century, very few changes occurred in the basic publishing agreement between authors and publishers. Escalating royalty clauses were the rule, with the author's share usually sliding from 10 percent to 12.5 percent to 15 percent as sales figures rose. A few best-selling authors were able to command a straight 20 percent royalty on trade sales from the first copy sold, but such arrangements were infrequent. One finds variations not in royalty arrangements but in percentages of subsidiary rights and precise descriptions of those rights. A standard Scribners contract in the early 1920s simply stated that subsidiary money "shall be divided equally between said PUBLISHERS and said AUTHOR." There was no mention of bonus clauses or of advertising budgets.[47] In a 1938 contract with Harper and Brothers for *Children of God,* however, Vardis Fisher's agent was able to negotiate one scale of regular royalties for the novel and a higher scale if the book should win the Harper Prize Novel contest for 1938–39. Fisher was guaranteed a forty-five-hundred-dollar advertising budget on the first ten thousand copies printed and twenty-five cents advertising on each copy sold between ten thousand and twenty thousand. Fisher kept all abridgment, radio, and motion picture rights (though he needed the publisher's consent to sell or exercise them). By 1955 Fisher was able to command a straight 15 percent royalty from Doubleday for his novel *Pemmican.* He received a six-thousand-dollar advance and kept all foreign rights for himself. Surprisingly, Doubleday agreed to retain only 10 percent of movie, radio, and television rights—probably because it felt that Fisher's novel had little potential for adaptation to those media.[48]

One often finds evidence of sparring over subsidiary rights in the contracts for mystery novels, many of which had good prospects for radio or movie adaptation, even when they were not especially well written.

---

inspired by *A Farewell to Arms* (written by Allie Wrubel and Abner Silver) is listed in an Ampersand Books catalog, July 1984. There is information about the song based on *Of Time and the River* in the Scribner Archive (Wolfe files) at Princeton University. See Herbert E. Marks to Perkins, 6 August 1935. Wolfe received a courtesy payment of fifty dollars, three cents per copy on the sheet music, and one-third of all other revenues.

47. See, for example, the contracts for *This Side of Paradise* and *The Beautiful and Damned* facsimiled in appendix 9 of Matthew J. Bruccoli, *F. Scott Fitzgerald: A Descriptive Bibliography* (Pittsburgh: University of Pittsburgh Press, 1972).

48. These contracts are in the Fisher Collection, Elizabeth Nowell files, Beinecke Library, Yale University, New Haven, Conn.

Ideally, publishers wanted an equal division of subsidiary income with the author, but by midcentury, authors had begun to insist, through their agents, on more favorable splits—60 percent/40 percent and even 75 percent/25 percent in their favor. In a 1943 contract for a forgettable parlor mystery called *Death and Bitters,* Sarah Thorson (who wrote under the pseudonym Kit Christian) agreed to split fifty-fifty with E. P. Dutton on digest, abridgment, anthology, book club, second serial, reprint edition, and syndication rights. However, Thorson kept three-fourths of first serial, movie, drama, radio, television, British, and translation rights.[49] Her contract is typical of many others of the 1940s and 1950s: subsidiary rights are described much more specifically (moving picture rights, for instance, are carefully differentiated from television rights), and authors retain higher percentages of these rights.

Since 1950, successful authors have recycled their work in the same ways that Fitzgerald, Hemingway, and Steinbeck did. A good example is James Dickey. Before publication of his novel *Deliverance* in 1971, Dickey was known as a promising poet. He had issued four collections of verse from 1960 to 1965; two years later he published a collected volume, *Poems, 1957–1967,* with Wesleyan University Press. His academic reputation was high, and he was well known on the poetry-reading circuit, but his income from published writings was, by his own testimony, negligible. He depended on academic appointments and, for a time, on a stipend from the Library of Congress for his major support. *Deliverance,* however, changed his career.

It is no longer common practice for an author to serialize an entire novel before publication in several issues of a magazine. Today usually only a portion of the book—which literary agents call a "teaser"—is pre-published. *Deliverance* was handled in this fashion: one of the most violent and exciting passages was published in the February 1970 issue of the *Atlantic Monthly,* and the clothbound book went on sale shortly thereafter. Both Book-of-the-Month Club and, later, Literary Guild offered *Deliverance* to their subscribers; after that, the novel had wide sales as a Dell paperback and is still taught from this softbound text in college courses. Movie rights were sold to Warner Brothers for six figures; Dickey himself collaborated on the screenplay for an additional fee. The author even managed to land a part in the film version as a slow-talking Southern sheriff. Paperback sales of *Deliverance* have been steady, but the big

49. The contract is in the Holly Collection.

money from its recycling probably has been earned. Dickey still includes a passage from the book in his public readings, however—a chilling sequence that captures an audience's attention. For years Dickey has been one of the highest-paid authors on the lecture circuit; a percentage of each honorarium check derives from *Deliverance,* which he composed years ago and which continues to yield income for him.

Dickey's friend William Styron has realized income on his writings in the same ways, with some variations. Portions of *Sophie's Choice* were pre-published in *Esquire;* the book sold in hardback through Random House and Book-of-the-Month Club; Bantam acquired paperback rights for $1,575,000, of which $500,000 went to Random House; motion picture rights went to Keith Barish for $650,000. Styron's work is read and appreciated throughout Europe, especially in France. Translations and British rights have therefore brought significant income to him. Ten years ago, fees from foreign publishers for translations were relatively small— somewhere in the range of $1,500 to $5,000, depending on the country. But for *Sophie's Choice* the British rights brought $200,000, French rights another $200,000, and German rights $100,000.[50]

To a student of the modern literary marketplace, the mention of subsidiary rights calls up images of million-dollar movie deals, cable television tie-ins, novelizations of film scripts, and the entire blockbuster mentality of current publishing. It is important to realize, however, that these tendencies in American publishing did not come about overnight or recently. They resulted instead from efforts by American authors and publishers over the past 150 years to realize the maximum earning potential of literary property. Longfellow, Howells, Atherton, Fitzgerald, and O'Neill would not be surprised to see current publishers' contracts with clauses on toy, T-shirt, and video-game rights. They would know that the ways in which a literary work can be made to yield profit are limited only by the ingenuity of those who control it.

50. Styron to West, 19 March 1983.

Chapter 8

Blockbusters

The book industry always needs a menace.

—O. H. Cheney (1931)

Since 1950 there have been major changes in the structure, ownership, and financing of the book industry in the United States. The situation should be familiar by now to anyone who is interested in current literature; indeed, it is hardly possible not to have heard about these conflicts in publishing, even if one reads only the newspapers. Briefly the situation is this: over the last twenty years, ownership of nearly all major American trade houses has fallen into the hands of conglomerates. This shift has altered the structure of authority and accountability within the publishing industry. Many houses are now pebbles in huge conglomerates, and one frequently hears it said that the profit margin is all that matters. Authors of serious books are said to be worried, as are publishers who wish to see themselves as intellectuals or cultural arbiters. What effect will a predominantly business mentality have on publishing? Will unprofitable or marginal types of publishing—experimental fiction, biography, history, and belles lettres—die out entirely? [1]

Other factors complicate the picture. Since World War II, the relationship between paperback and hardcover publishing has changed. Paperback houses now control much of the market and influence virtually all decisions about the publication, promotion, and distribution of books. The neighborhood bookstore has almost vanished because of the emergence of chain outlets like B. Dalton and Waldenbooks. These outlets, usually located in shopping centers or other high-traffic areas, deal in volume. They emphasize quick-turnover best-sellers, frequently offered at discount prices, and are set up to encourage impulse buying. Their cash registers are wired into central computers, their inventories are carefully

---

1. Recent studies of the book industry include Thomas Whiteside, *The Blockbuster Complex: Conglomerates, Show Business, and Book Publishing* (Middletown, Conn.: Wesleyan University Press, 1981); Leonard Shatzkin, *In Cold Type* (Boston: Houghton Mifflin, 1982); and Lewis A. Coser, Charles Kadushin, and Walter W. Powell, *Books: The Culture and Commerce of Publishing* (New York: Basic Books, 1982).

controlled, and they stock only what will sell. There is no room for slow titles from a publisher's backlist.

Agents wield more power on the literary marketplace today than they did formerly, largely because the possibilities for recycling a modern best-seller have become so numerous: magazine serialization or excerpting, hardback publication, book clubs, paperback sales, abridged or digest publication, movie rights, television rights, translation rights, drama rights, and other ancillary rights. Ideally the entire campaign for a best-seller should be orchestrated by an agent and a publisher in such a way as to attain maximum exposure and sales. The author is important in these promotional efforts: he or she must be willing to go on tour, appear on television talk shows, attend autograph parties, and be available and agreeable to the media. If the campaign works, the author is handsomely rewarded—but, of course, it does not always work.

Publishing is a high-risk business that involves a strong element of gambling. All publishers gamble, but they must be able to back their wagers with predictable lines of textbooks, juvenile titles, cookbooks, encyclopedias, or religious titles. Cash flow has always been a problem, particularly in a slow season, and venture capital has in the past been fairly scarce. Publishers interested primarily in making money can cut some of the risks by concentrating on those books that are sure to sell. They can publish volumes conceived to meet a particular need and appeal to a predictable market—reference tools and technical manuals, for example. Though the profits in this kind of publishing are not great, the hazards are relatively small. The excitement and quick profits are in high-risk areas, however—popular fiction, investigative reporting, public personalities, and current events. And the economics are such that a publisher's investment on a potential blockbuster is very small compared to what can be earned if the book is a success. The key is to select the best-seller ahead of time, but no one has been able to do that with regularity.

The consequent strategy employed by some publishers is to overproduce: to publish more titles than one's firm can hope to market successfully, then choose the three or four that attract the best initial response and throw the entire weight of one's promotional efforts behind them. If a book does not respond, the publisher should stop advertising it and bring in an alternate from the wings. One winner, with its golden spin-offs and subsidiary rights, should put the firm in black ink for the season.

In the view of many people in the industry, this approach to publishing is not in the best interests of the serious author. Traditionally, such an author has been thought to need a patient publisher with enough financial muscle to absorb losses on, say, the first three books. By then the author should have built a large enough reputation and readership to make a success on the fourth volume. The previous books, if they have been kept alive on the backlist, may then start to move. By the fifth book the author should have a substantial following, and the publisher should own a group of valuable literary properties. At best—as with Sinclair Lewis, John Steinbeck, and Saul Bellow—this kind of success and recognition comes around the middle of a writer's career. But many authors (William Faulkner and James Agee come to mind) do not live to enjoy very much of their success, though their publishers and heirs certainly benefit from it.

Publishers today, we are told, do not look very far into the future. Influenced by MBAs placed in accounting departments and management positions by conglomerate owners, American trade publishers are said to emphasize short-term profits, quick sales, and a brief life on the backlist. Firms now publish individual books, not authors, because the chances are that agents will keep their authors moving from house to house in search of even larger advances and royalties. If a publisher loses on one book by an author, the publisher cannot expect to recoup on the next book because by then the author will have moved to another firm.

It is difficult to know how much to believe of what one hears and reads. What may actually be important is not how much is true but how much is accepted and acted upon as truth. Perhaps one should not take an alarmist view too readily. What is happening in the book industry is also happening in a number of related business fields, and behind these developments are broad economic and social forces. The difficulties in publishing did not come about overnight in 1959 when Random House went public. The problems are actually quite venerable; they can be found in one form or another as far back as the eighteenth century in England, and the current crisis is similar to upheavals in American publishing that have taken place periodically since about 1870. These conflicts are inherent in book publishing; they are the product of natural tensions within the industry, and they will probably never go away. In some respects, they may even be healthy.

What has happened to publishing over the last twenty years is similar to what has taken place in two related mass-culture industries—motion pictures and popular music. The old Hollywood studio system, in which each major company kept a group of stars under contract, has given way to an independent, free-wheeling environment in which major stars and directors move from studio to studio. Like publishing houses, motion picture studios produce more movies than the market can accommodate and then choose to support only those films that seem most likely to be hits. A movie has from three to six weeks (at most) to demonstrate its drawing power. If it makes a poor initial showing at the box office, it is withdrawn and a substitute is brought in. Movie producers gamble in the same ways that publishers do; the only difference is that the stakes and potential winnings are higher. Many of the major studios are now under the wings of conglomerates—often the same ones that control publishing houses. It is difficult to generalize, but the effect on American movies has probably been negative. The appeal today seems most often to be pitched low. Good films still appear, but much of the time the theaters are filled with ghoulish sex thrillers and macho adventure fantasies. These are apparently the safest bets.

The pop record industry resembles publishing even more closely. The business runs on hype, and the half-life of a single on the racks is quite short. Groups move from label to label, and contract disputes fill the trade papers. Record executives, like publishers and movie moguls, gamble with conglomerate money; they keep rolling the dice and hope that eventually a winner will turn up. Here again, the effect on the product seems to have been bad. Mass tastes change, of course, but yesterday's disco hits and today's synthesized pop hardly measure up to what rockers of the fifties and sixties used to produce. Good popular artists and groups do survive and record, however, and the existence of a highly developed apparatus for promotion and distribution has allowed them to reach large audiences.

Among entertainment industries the closest parallel to what has happened in book publishing can probably be found in professional basketball. The situations are quite similar and the correspondences interesting. The old National Basketball Association was dominated by paternalistic owners whose teams were often their only businesses. Many teams were family operations, owned through two or three generations. Major revenues came from gate receipts and concessions. Production was about right for the market: there were eight teams, and the level of talent on each was high. Players dealt directly with owners in contract matters, and a player often spent his entire career with one team. He put in an apprenticeship during which he learned the game and the team absorbed his mistakes. Later he might move into a starring role, and when his playing days were finished, he often stayed with the team in some front-office capacity or became a businessman in the community.

The old-time NBA coach was a teacher. He did not assume that his rookies came to him with fully developed skills; rather, he taught them the professional game and tried to bring them along slowly. The NBA featured genuine rivalries and thrived on the loyalty of knowledgeable fans in cities like New York, Chicago, Boston, St. Louis, and Philadelphia. At its best, professional basketball embodied important American values—the rewards of hard work, team play, dedication, and loyalty. The best players became folk heroes.

Today's game, by contrast, is more show business than sport. Many current NBA owners are millionaires who have made quick money elsewhere and have purchased pro teams for ego gratification and tax write-offs. Teams change hands frequently. After two or three years the tax advantages diminish, and the pleasure of associating with famous athletes apparently wears off. Revenues come partly from the gate and the concession stand, but the significant money now comes from television rights, from steep fees paid by expansion teams to enter the league, and from tax advantages. Players deal with owners through agents, and the best players (rookies and veterans alike) have no-cut contracts with large advances and incentive clauses. Players have become commodities. Because many of them move from team to team, they build few loyalties with the organizations or fans for whom they play. The league has probably been damaged by overproduction: there are now twenty-five teams, talent is thinly spread, team chemistry is often poor. The pro season is long, the travel schedule exhausting, and the pace of play numbing.

Players today are expected to be entertainers as well as athletes, and they are often victimized by the modern cult of personality and media hype. The availability of television dollars has sent salaries soaring and has stimulated the greed of players and owners alike. Professional basketball still embodies American themes, but often they are bad ones now: the bad effects of big money and quick fame on impressionable young men from minority groups, the packaging of a mass-culture event as something it is not.

Will the same thing happen to publishing? The factors that have damaged professional basketball are similar to those that have altered the publishing industry: ownership by people who do not understand the business fully, overproduction and consequent dilution of talent, the influx of big money from subsidiary rights, agents as a negotiating force, the absence of loyalty in employer-employee relationships, the influence of media fame, the tendency to buy already developed talent rather than to bring up young talent through an apprentice system, the tendency of sportswriters (like book critics) to concentrate on image and personality rather than on acquired skill.[2]

One hopes that publishing, a very old business, will not go the way of professional basketball, a very young one. To acquire a proper perspective, it may be useful to take an economic view. These problems are not new in the American economy. In any capitalistic enterprise there are natural tensions between popular and elitist forces. Put very crudely, one can try to sell a large number of items at a low unit price to a mass market, or one can attempt to sell fewer items at a high price to a limited market. The latter approach requires cooperation among producers. High prices in a limited market will work for a time, especially if the economy is down, but in recent American history the pressure of technology, exerted through new and better mass-production methods, has periodically forced manufacturers to address larger markets. This has happened several times in publishing, and each time an old guard has mounted a vigorous campaign to defeat, or at least weaken, the pressure of the mass market. Small-scale publishing, they argue, is in the long run about as profitable as mass-market publishing, and it is much simpler and more dignified. By addressing a geographically concentrated and culturally homogeneous market, the publisher can minimize distribution and fulfillment problems and predict more accurately what will sell. The operation will be smaller, the prices higher, the overhead lower, the print runs shorter, the remainder stock less numerous. Just as important, publishers will be able to think of themselves as professionals rather than merchants, intellectuals rather than purveyors of popular culture.

These struggles have been going on for many years in the American publishing industry. In 1870, for example, publishing in America was a stable and relatively profitable business operated along elitist lines. The

2. For an economic analysis of the NBA, see David Halberstam, *The Breaks of the Game* (New York: Knopf, 1981), pp. 10–15.

established houses adhered, more or less faithfully, to the principle of courtesy of the trade. Into this situation came a group of early paperback publishers, who pirated British authors freely, produced books in great quantity, and sold them in large numbers through nontraditional outlets. They were able to do so because of the development of power-driven cylinder presses, new mechanical typesetters, stereotype plating, cheap wood-pulp paper, and improved folding and casing methods. These publishers undercut the established houses and deprived them of income. A few old-line publishers responded by issuing their own lines of cheap books, but most sat back, complained in the trade journals, and attempted to persuade Congress to kill off the mavericks by passing new tax and postal regulations. None of these strategies worked, and the paperback publishers flourished for about fifteen years. They were finally ruined by their own overproduction, by passage of the international copyright law of 1891, and by a major business panic in 1893. These paperback houses perished, but they had shown American publishers that it was possible to reach the mass market and that the market was ready. The established houses responded by returning to conservative approaches and staying away from paperback publishing and mass distribution for the next fifty years.[3]

As we have seen in chapter 2, a second crisis came about in 1901. Macy's department store in New York City refused to alter its policy of featuring clothbound best-sellers as loss leaders. By marketing these books below retail, Macy's undercut independent booksellers and threatened the stability of the price structure in the industry. Publishers reacted by refusing to sell net books to Macy's, and the department store had to lodge suits against the American Publishers Association and the American Booksellers Association—suits that it eventually won—in order to sell books at a discount.

In 1926, Harry Scherman and Maxwell Sackheim founded the Book-of-the-Month Club, and later that year Doubleday began the Literary Guild. Both clubs reached markets that established publishers had never attempted to tap. The book clubs prospered because the market was ready, but instead of cooperating with these clubs, trade houses tried to

3. Frank Luther Mott, *Golden Multitudes: The Story of Best Sellers in the United States* (New York: Macmillan, 1947), pp. 148–55; Charles A. Madison, *Book Publishing in America* (New York: McGraw-Hill, 1966), pp. 50–60; John Tebbel, *A History of Book Publishing in the United States*, 4 vols. (New York: Bowker, 1972–81), 2:481–511; Madeleine B. Stern, ed., *Publishers for Mass Entertainment in the Nineteenth Century* (Boston: G. K. Hall, 1980).

kill them off. Influential persons like John Macrae (president of E. P. Dutton and Co.), John W. Hiltman (head of D. Appleton and Co.), and Arthur Brentano, Jr. (president of the American Booksellers Association) attacked the clubs vehemently for standardizing mass tastes and interfering with the status quo. Macrae's published remarks were so vitriolic that BOMC finally brought suit against him in May 1929 for libel, asking two hundred thousand dollars in damages. A settlement was effected by Richard Fuller, vice-president of the ABA; Macrae issued a retraction in August, and BOMC withdrew its suit. But the lines had been drawn and the tone of the relationship established. The book clubs would be quite successful, but for the next twenty-five years they would frequently come under fire. In July 1951, for example, the booksellers set the Federal Trade Commission on them, charging that exclusive plate-leasing to book clubs by publishers constituted a monopolistic practice. The FTC ruled in favor of the clubs in September 1953. Eventually book-club sales and advertising became so important to publishers, however, that they learned to be more cooperative. Selection of a title by a major book club guaranteed that it would make money as a hardback and helped raise the prices fetched by its subsidiary rights. Trade houses learned to coexist with book clubs, but it took many years for a proper level of cooperation to be reached.[4]

Spokesmen for the traditionalists in publishing have always been active and articulate, and their arguments have changed little over the past eighty years. As one investigates the history of the twentieth-century American book trade, one is struck by the currency of the disputes. Here, for example, is a quotation from the lead editorial in the *Dial* for 16 May 1900. The piece is entitled "The Star System in Publishing":

> Many worthy books are neglected in order that a few may be kept well to the front. When the caprice is past, when the serried ranks of worn copies of "Trilby" gather dust upon the shelves of the public library, when the unsold copies in the hands of the publisher and bookseller become "plugs," the publisher should then know better than to complain because his other books do not sell. The fact often is that he has not tried to sell them, that he has left them unadvertised and uncared-for, that they have now lost their chance because his "enterprise" has seen fit to promote the sale of a few books at the expense of all the rest. The well-advised publisher, in our opinion, is the one who recognizes

4. Charles Lee, *The Hidden Public: The Story of the Book-of-the-Month Club* (Garden City, N.Y.: Doubleday, 1958), pp. 44–59, 95–100; Madison, *Book Publishing in America*, pp. 393–94.

the evils of the star system, and is not misled by its promise of present temporary gain.

Henry Holt, writing in 1905, might have been referring to conditions during the 1970s and 1980s:

> Not as many books pay for themselves as did before; but the few that do sell, sell more widely, and thus may still do their share to pay the losses and expenses on the rest. Hence the mad quest of the golden seller, the mad payment to the man who has once produced it, and the mad advertising of doubtful books in the hope of creating the seller,—by pictures, dummies, big letters and other methods fit only for candy, whiskey, tobacco, and other articles of unlimited sale. All this reacts, as has been explained, to crush out all books but the seller.[5]

The points made by Henry Mills Alden of Harper and Brothers sound quite current, though he is writing in 1908:

> It is within our memory that the only factors in the business of publication were the author, the publisher, the bookseller, and the reader. Of these, the old-fashioned bookseller, who knew and intelligently appreciated the books he handled, has been driven to the wall, and the mechanical system which has taken his place is blind to every value he recognized and eagerly aware of those values which to him had no significance, but which have now come to the front, determining through indiscriminate advertisement the choice of a fickle multitude of book-buyers. The record of big sales is paraded as in itself a certificate of merit. The relation of the publisher to author and reader has lost much of its former frankness and simplicity. The literary agent on the one side and the "trade" on the other seek to force his hand, and if they do not make him an out-and-out merchant, it is because he has uncommon virtues of resistance.[6]

These points are similar to those made by critics of the conglomerates today. One encounters these arguments in all decades of twentieth-century American publishing. George P. Brett of Macmillan used them in the nineteen-teens; W. W. Appleton employed them in the twenties; Maxwell Perkins repeated them in the thirties; Alfred R. McIntyre recycled them in the forties; John Farrar restated them in the fifties; Alfred A. Knopf used them during the sixties.[7] Conglomerates, in all

5. "The Commercialization of Literature," *Atlantic Monthly* 96 (Nov. 1905): 599.

6. "Prizes of Authorship," in *Magazine Writing and the New Literature* (New York: Harpers, 1908), pp. 102–3.

7. George P. Brett, "Book-Publishing and Its Present Tendencies," *Atlantic Monthly* 111 (Apr. 1913): 454–62; Grant Overton, *Portrait of a Publisher: The First Hundred Years of the House of Appleton, 1825–1925* (New York: Appleton, 1925), pp. 22ff; John Hall Wheelock, ed.,

fairness, did not create the problems for which they are blamed. These problems were present all along and will probably always be present. Samuel Vaughan of Random House, who was quoted in chapter 4, on the trade editor, finds the current disputes familiar. "These conflicts and frictions in trade publishing are of long standing," he says. "I also happen to think that in many ways they are good. They give the business its energy."[8]

Conglomerate control has caused some problems, but it has also brought some positive developments. There is now more risk capital than there was formerly; houses actually need books in order to justify the high overhead expenses that most of them pay. Through their agents, successful writers have more power than before and are more likely to be informed about the marketing and distribution strategies used to sell their books. There are even a few good aspects to the hype. As with pop records, the existence of a highly developed marketing apparatus makes it possible for serious authors, if they can employ the system, to reach quite large audiences. Historically, book publishers have preferred to concentrate on limited markets, to charge high prices, and to enter the mass market only when forced to by economic pressures, technology, and competition. The situation in current publishing has required them to do so, and as a consequence many American authors are reaching wider, more geographically and demographically diverse audiences than before. And some authors are better paid than they used to be, a development one must applaud.

Certain things will probably never again be the same. Close relationships between authors and individual publishing houses—at least large trade houses—may be largely gone. The role of the editor has probably been irreversibly altered. The literary agent is more powerful now, and through the agent the author is stronger. The audience for which the serious author can write today is much wider and more interesting than it used to be.

These changes in contemporary publishing will certainly influence

Editor to Author: The Letters of Maxwell E. Perkins (New York: Scribners, 1950), pp. 73–74, 128, 138, 144, 168; Alfred R. McIntyre, "The Crisis in Book Publishing," *Atlantic Monthly* 180 (Oct. 1947): 107–10; John Farrar, "Publishing: Industry and Profession," *American Scholar* 19 (Winter 1949–50): 31–39; Alfred A. Knopf, *Some Random Recollections* (New York: The Typophiles, 1949); idem, *Publishing Then and Now, 1912–1964*, Twenty-first Bowker Lecture (New York: New York Public Library, 1964).

8. Interview with Samuel S. Vaughan, 22 September 1987.

American writers, and the eventual effect may not be altogether negative. Tensions between art and commerce will, as always, be passed through publishers and agents to authors. If serious literary authors begin to feel that they can reach real audiences—that through the publishing industry they can communicate with a sizable group of readers—they may rediscover some of the lessons that authors from Shakespeare to Dickens to Fitzgerald have absorbed. Literature, if it is to survive and have influence, must not be focused relentlessly inward. It must not be written for English professors or New York book critics. It must instead draw material and energy from the society around it, and it must have narrative drive and popular appeal. The conglomerate executives may not know it, but in the end they may be a force that helps give modern American literature the broad audience it has always needed but until now has had little chance of reaching.

Permissions

I am most grateful to the various libraries at which I have done archival research during the preparation of this book. For permission to publish information from the Random House Collection and from the Paul Revere Reynolds, Harold Ober, and Curtis Brown Collections I thank the Rare Book and Manuscript Division of the Butler Library, Columbia University. Comments by Harry Scherman concerning the Book-of-the-Month Club are published with the permission of the Oral History Collection, Butler Library. Materials from the Charles Scribner's Sons and Henry Holt Archives and from the Booth Tarkington Papers at Princeton are published with the permission of Princeton University Library. Quotations from the Macmillan Company Records and from the Flora May Holly Papers appear with the permission of the Rare Book and Manuscript Division, The New York Public Library, Astor, Lenox and Tilden Foundations. Letters from the Papers of Ellen Glasgow are published with permission from the Manuscript Department, University of Virginia Library. Quotations from the literary papers of Eugene O'Neill, Sinclair Lewis, Vardis Fisher, Stephen Vincent Benét, and John P. Marquand are reproduced with the permission of the Collection of American Literature, Beinecke Rare Book and Manuscript Library, Yale University.

Grateful acknowledgment is made to Random House, Inc., for permission to publish quotations from four Bennett Cerf letters and one Robert Linscott letter in the Random House Collection, Butler Library. A letter from George Brett to Edna Ferber is quoted with permission from the Macmillan Publishing Company, New York. Quotations from Alfred Harcourt's letters to Ellen Glasgow are used with the permission of Harcourt Brace Jovanovich, Inc. Unpublished letters of Maxwell Perkins and Robert Bridges and other materials from the Scribner Archive at Princeton University Library are quoted with permission from Charles Scribner's Sons. All rights reserved. Frederick Macmillan's comment on Curtis Brown is published with the permission of Macmillan Publishers Ltd., London. Excerpts from the letters of Henry Holt to Paul Revere Reynolds and S. S. McClure are published courtesy of

Henry Holt and Co., Inc. Permission to quote from a Nelson Doubleday letter to Ellen Glasgow has been granted by Doubleday & Co., Inc.

A letter from Alan C. Collins to W. H. Auden is excerpted with the permission of Curtis Brown Ltd. Letters from Ogden Nash to his literary agents are quoted with the permission of the Ogden Nash estate. Quotations from three letters written by Carl Brandt to Stephen Vincent Benét are used with permission from Brandt and Brandt, Literary Agents, Inc. Editorial correspondence from Adelaide W. Neall to Booth Tarkington is used with the permission of *The Saturday Evening Post,* The Curtis Publishing Co., Indianapolis. Hugh M. Kahler's letter to Carl Brandt is quoted courtesy of *Ladies' Home Journal.* A quotation from a letter from Goldwyn Production Corporation to Henry Holt is published with permission from The Samuel Goldwyn Company, Los Angeles.

Paul Gallico's letters to Harold Ober are quoted with the permission of Virginia Gallico. Conrad Aiken's letter to Maxwell Perkins is excerpted with the permission of Mrs. Conrad Aiken. Quotations from an Ida Tarbell letter to Paul Revere Reynolds are published with the permission of Caroline Tarbell Tupper. Sinclair Lewis's letters to B. W. Huebsch and to Nelson Doubleday are quoted with the permission of the Estate of Sinclair Lewis, c/o Ernst, Cane, Berner & Gitlin, Counsellors at Law, New York. Permission to publish quotations from William Saroyan's letters to Random House has been granted by the William Saroyan Foundation, San Francisco. Excerpts from the letters of Edna Ferber are Copyright © 1988 by Harriet F. Pilpel as executrix of the Estate of Edna Ferber and as Trustee. John P. Marquand's cable to Carl Brandt is quoted with the kind permission of John P. Marquand, Jr. Quotations from two letters by W. H. Auden to Bennett Cerf are printed with the permission of The Estate of W. H. Auden, Edward Mendelson, Literary Executor. A portion of Gertrude Atherton's letter to George Brett is quoted with the permission of her granddaughter, Florence Atherton Dickey. Quotations from letters by James M. Cain to Mrs. William Donahey and to Cyril Clemens are published courtesy of Alice M. Piper. Quotations from interviews with Robert D. Loomis and Samuel S. Vaughan, both of Random House, Inc., are used with the kind permission of those two gentlemen.

Material in several of the chapters appeared earlier in these scholarly journals: *Review,* the *Harvard Library Bulletin,* the *Yale University Library Gazette,* and the *National Humanities Center Newsletter.* I am grateful to these journals for permission to reprint these sections.

For information rather than quotations, I thank the following persons, who shared their knowledge of the literary marketplace with me: Dan Lawrence of McGraw-Hill, William Koshland of A. A. Knopf, Inc., Don Congdon and Elizabeth McKee, both then of Harold Matson Co., Inc., and literary agent Bertha Klausner.

Bibliography

Most of the references below are to works of publishing history. Standard literary histories, literary biographies, editions of correspondence, and reference works have not been cited. Important book-length studies and some of the articles mentioned in the footnotes are included here as well.

BOOKS

Allen, Frederick Lewis. *Paul Revere Reynolds*. New York: privately published, 1944.

Anderson, Charles B., ed. *Bookselling in America and the World*. New York: Quadrangle/The New York Times Book Co., 1975.

Anesko, Michael. *"Friction with the Market": Henry James and the Profession of Authorship*. New York: Oxford University Press, 1986.

At Random: The Reminiscences of Bennett Cerf. New York: Random House, 1977.

Bailey, Herbert S., Jr. *The Art and Science of Book Publishing*. New York: Harper and Row, 1970.

Ballou, Ellen B. *The Building of the House: Houghton Mifflin's Formative Years*. Boston: Houghton Mifflin, 1970.

Barnes, James J. *Authors, Publishers and Politicians: The Quest for an Anglo-American Copyright Agreement, 1815–1854*. London: Routledge and Kegan Paul, 1974.

Berg, A. Scott. *Max Perkins: Editor of Genius*. New York: E. P. Dutton, 1978.

Bernheim, Alfred L. *The Business of the Theatre: An Economic History of the American Theatre, 1750–1932*. New York: Benjamin Blom, Inc., 1964.

Bonham-Carter, Victor. *Authors by Profession*. 2 vols. Los Altos, Calif.: William Kaufmann, 1978, 1984.

Bowker Lectures on Book Publishing. New York: Bowker, 1957.

Brown, Curtis. *Contacts*. London: Cassell, 1935.

Brownell, Gertrude Hall, ed. *William Crary Brownell: An Anthology of His Writings together with Notes and Impressions of Later Years*. New York: Scribners, 1933.

Bryant, Keith L., Jr., and Henry C. Dethloff. *A History of American Business*. Englewood Cliffs, N.J.: Prentice-Hall, 1983.

Burlingame, Roger. *Endless Frontiers: The Story of McGraw-Hill*. New York: McGraw-Hill, 1959.

———. *Of Making Many Books*. New York: Scribners, 1946.

Charvat, William. *Literary Publishing in America, 1790–1850*. 1957–58 Rosenbach Lectures. Philadelphia: University of Pennsylvania Press, 1959.

———. *The Profession of Authorship in America, 1800–1870*. Columbus: Ohio State University Press, 1968.

Cheney, O. H. *Economic Survey of the Book Industry, 1930–1931.* National Association of Book Publishers, 1931. Reprint. New York: Bowker, 1960.

Cochran, Thomas C. *Business in American Life: A History.* New York: McGraw-Hill, 1972.

Commins, Dorothy. *What Is an Editor? Saxe Commins at Work.* Chicago: University of Chicago Press, 1978.

Compaine, Benjamin M. *The Book Industry in Transition: An Economic Study of Book Distribution and Marketing.* White Plains, N.Y.: Knowledge Industry Publications, 1978.

Coser, Lewis A., Charles Kadushin, and Walter W. Powell. *Books: The Culture and Commerce of Publishing.* New York: Basic Books, 1982.

Crider, Allen Billy, ed. *Mass Market Publishing in America.* Boston: G. K. Hall, 1982.

Cross, Nigel. *The Common Writer: Life in Nineteenth-Century Grub Street.* Cambridge: Cambridge University Press, 1985.

Dessauer, John P. *Book Publishing: What It Is, What It Does.* New York: Bowker, 1974.

Doran, George H. *Chronicles of Barabbas, 1884–1934.* London: Methuen, 1935.

Emery, Edwin. *History of the American Newspaper Publishers Association.* 1950. Reprint. Westport, Conn.: Greenwood Press, 1970.

Exman, Eugene. *The Brothers Harper.* New York: Harper and Row, 1965.

———. *The House of Harper: One Hundred and Fifty Years of Publishing.* New York: Harper and Row, 1967.

Fensch, Thomas. *Steinbeck and Covici, The Story of a Friendship.* Middlebury, Vt.: Paul S. Eriksson, 1979.

Fleming, E. McClung. *R. R. Bowker: Militant Liberal.* Norman: University of Oklahoma Press, 1952.

Foley, Martha. *The Story of Story Magazine: A Memoir.* Ed. with an intro. and afterword by Jay Neugeboren. New York: Norton, 1980.

Gilmer, Walker. *Horace Liveright: Publisher of the Twenties.* New York: David Lewis, 1970.

Grannis, Chandler B., ed. *What Happens in Book Publishing.* 2d ed. New York: Columbia University Press, 1967.

Gross, Gerald, ed. *Editors on Editing.* New York: Bowker, 1961. Rev. ed. New York: Harper and Row, 1985.

———, ed. *Publishers on Publishing.* New York: Bowker, 1961.

Haldeman-Julius, E. *The First Hundred Million.* New York: Simon and Schuster, 1928.

Harper, J. Henry. *The House of Harper: A Century of Publishing in Franklin Square.* New York: Harper and Bros., 1912.

Haydn, Hiram. *Words and Faces.* New York: Harcourt Brace Jovanovich, 1974.

Henderson, Bill, ed. *The Art of Literary Publishing: Editors on Their Craft.* Wainscott, N.Y.: Pushcart Press, 1980.

Hepburn, James. *The Author's Empty Purse and the Rise of the Literary Agent.* London: Oxford University Press, 1968.

Howard, William J., ed. *Editor, Author, and Publisher: Papers Given at the Editorial Conference, University of Toronto, November 1968.* Toronto: University of Toronto Press, 1969.

Jovanovich, William. *Now, Barabbas*. New York: Harper and Row, 1964.

Kazin, Alfred, Dan Lacy, and Ernest L. Boyer. *The State of the Book World, 1980: Three Talks Sponsored by The Center for the Book in the Library of Congress*. Washington, D.C.: Library of Congress, 1981.

Kingston, Paul William, and Jonathan R. Cole. *The Wages of Writing: Per Word, Per Piece, or Perhaps*. New York: Columbia University Press, 1986.

Knopf, Alfred A. *Publishing Then and Now, 1912–1964*. Twenty-first Bowker Lecture. New York: New York Public Library, 1964.

———. *Some Random Recollections*. New York: The Typophiles, 1949.

Lane, Michael, with Jeremy Booth. *Books and Publishers: Commerce against Culture in Postwar Britain*. Lexington, Mass.: Lexington Books, 1980.

Lee, Charles. *The Hidden Public: The Story of the Book-of-the-Month Club*. Garden City, N.Y.: Doubleday, 1958.

Lehmann-Haupt, Hellmut, in collab. with Lawrence C. Wroth and Rollo G. Silver. *The Book in America: A History of the Making and Selling of Books in the United States*. 2d ed. New York: Bowker, 1951.

Link, Henry C., and Harry Arthur Hopf. *People and Books: A Study of Reading and Book Buying Habits*. New York: Book Manufacturers' Inst., 1946.

Literary Agents: A Complete Guide. New York: Poets and Writers, Inc., 1978.

Madison, Charles A. *Book Publishing in America*. New York: McGraw-Hill, 1966.

———. *Irving to Irving: Author-Publisher Relations, 1800–1974*. New York: Bowker, 1974.

Mayes, Herbert R. *The Magazine Maze: A Prejudiced Perspective*. Garden City, N.Y.: Doubleday, 1980.

Miller, Edwin H. *The Professional Writer in Elizabethan England*. Cambridge: Harvard University Press, 1959.

Miller, William. *The Book Industry*. New York: Columbia University Press, 1949.

Mitchell, Burroughs. *The Education of an Editor*. Garden City, N.Y.: Doubleday, 1980.

Mott, Frank Luther. *Golden Multitudes: The Story of Best Sellers in the United States*. New York: Macmillan, 1947.

Overton, Grant. *Portrait of a Publisher: The First Hundred Years of the House of Appleton, 1825–1925*. New York: Appleton, 1925.

[Page, Walter Hines]. *A Publisher's Confession*. New York: Doubleday, Page and Co., 1905.

Patten, Robert L. *Charles Dickens and His Publishers*. Oxford: Clarendon Press, 1978.

Peterson, Theodore. *Magazines in the Twentieth Century*. 2d ed. Urbana: University of Illinois Press, 1964.

Plant, Marjorie. *The English Book Trade: An Economic History of the Making and Sale of Books*. 3d ed. London: Allen and Unwin, 1974.

Poggi, Jack. *Theater in America: The Impact of Economic Forces, 1870–1967*. Ithaca, N.Y.: Cornell University Press, 1968.

Putnam, George Haven, and J. Bishop Putnam. *Authors and Publishers*. 7th ed. New York: Putnam, 1897.

Reynolds, Paul R. *The Middle Man: The Adventures of a Literary Agent*. New York: William Morrow, 1972.

Saunders, J. W. *The Profession of English Letters*. London: Routledge and Kegan Paul, 1964.

Schick, Frank L. *The Paperbound Book in America*. New York: Bowker, 1958.

Shatzkin, Leonard. *In Cold Type*. Boston: Houghton Mifflin, 1982.

Sheehan, Donald. *This Was Publishing: A Chronicle of the Book Trade in the Gilded Age*. Bloomington: Indiana University Press, 1952.

Simpson, Lewis P. *The Man of Letters in New England and the South: Essays on the History of the Literary Vocation in America*. Baton Rouge: Louisiana State University Press, 1973.

Stern, Madeleine B. *Imprints on History: Book Publishing and American Frontiers*. 1956. Reprint. New York: AMS Press, 1972.

———, ed. *Publishers for Mass Entertainment in the Nineteenth Century*. Boston: G. K. Hall, 1980.

Sutherland, J. A. *Fiction and the Fiction Industry*. London: Athlone Press, 1978.

Sutton, Walter. *The Western Book Trade: Cincinnati as a Nineteenth-Century Publishing and Book-Trade Center*. Columbus: Ohio State University Press, 1961.

Tebbel, John. *George Horace Lorimer and the* Saturday Evening Post. Garden City, N.Y.: Doubleday, 1948.

———. *A History of Book Publishing in the United States*. 4 vols. New York: Bowker, 1972–81.

Unseld, Siegfried. *The Author and His Publisher*. Translated by Hunter Hannum and Hildegarde Hannum. Chicago: University of Chicago Press, 1980.

Unwin, Stanley. *The Truth about Publishing*. London: Allen and Unwin, 1926. Rev. eds. 1946, 1960, 1976.

Watson, Graham. *Book Society*. London: Andre Deutsch, 1980.

Wheelock, John Hall, ed. *Editor to Author: The Letters of Maxwell E. Perkins*. New York: Scribners, 1950.

Whiteside, Thomas. *The Blockbuster Complex: Conglomerates, Show Business, and Book Publishing*. Middletown, Conn.: Wesleyan University Press, 1981.

Wilson, Christopher P. *The Labor of Words: Literary Professionalism in the Progressive Era*. Athens: University of Georgia Press, 1985.

Wood, James Playsted. *The Curtis Magazines*. New York: Ronald Press, 1971.

———. *Magazines in the United States*. 2d ed. New York: Ronald Press, 1956.

ARTICLES

Apple, R. W., Jr. "The Gold Rush on Publishers' Row." *Saturday Review* 43 (8 Oct. 1960): 13ff.

Atherton, Gertrude. "Literary Merchandise." *New Republic* 3 (3 July 1915): 223–24.

Blum, Eleanor. "Paperback Book Publishing: A Survey of Content." *Journalism Quarterly* 36 (Fall 1959): 447–54.

Brett, George P. "Book-Publishing and Its Present Tendencies." *Atlantic Monthly* 111 (Apr. 1913): 454–62.

[Brown, Curtis.] "'The Commercialization of Literature' and the Literary Agent." *Bookman* 24 (Oct. 1906): 134–39.

Cockburn, Alexander, and James Ridgeway. "Can Writers Unite?" *Village Voice*, 7–13 Oct. 1981, pp. 1ff.

"The Confessions of a Literary Press Agent." *Bookman* 24 (Dec. 1906): 335–39.

DeVoto, Bernard. "Writing for Money." *Saturday Review of Literature* 16 (9 Oct. 1937): 4.

Eaton, Andrew J. "The American Movement for International Copyright, 1837–60." *Library Quarterly* 15 (Apr. 1945): 95–122.

Farmer, David. "The Bibliographical Potential of a 20th Century Literary Agent's Archive: The Pinker Papers." *Library Chronicle of the University of Texas,* n.s. 3 (Nov. 1970): 26–35.

Farrar, John. "Publishing: Industry and Profession." *American Scholar* 19 (Winter 1949–50): 31–39.

Fiedler, Leslie. "Literature and Lucre." *New York Times Book Review,* 31 May 1981, pp. 7, 47–48.

Firth, John. "James Pinker to James Joyce, 1915–1920." *Studies in Bibliography* 21 (1968): 205–24.

Fischer, John. "Myths about Publishing." *Harper's Magazine* 227 (July 1963): 14ff.

Fredeman, William E. "The Bibliographical Significance of a Publisher's Archive: The Macmillan Papers." *Studies in Bibliography* 23 (1970): 183–91.

Fuchs, Miriam. "Poet and Patron: Hart Crane and Otto Kahn." *Book Forum* 6 (1982): 45–51.

Gilreath, James. "The Benjamin Huebsch Imprint." *Papers of the Bibliographical Society of America* 73 (2d Qtr., 1979): 225–43.

Hellman, Geoffrey T. "Publisher" (three-part profile of A. A. Knopf). *New Yorker* 24 (20 and 27 Nov., 4 Dec. 1948).

Holt, Henry. "The Commercialization of Literature: A Summing Up." *Putnam's Monthly* 2 (Feb. 1907): 563–75.

Kimball, Arthur Reed. "The Invasion of Journalism." *Atlantic Monthly* 86 (July 1900): 119–24.

Kleinfield, N. R. "The Literary Agent." *New York Times Book Review,* 7 Dec. 1980, pp. 9ff.

Klinkowitz, Jerome, and Karen Wood. "The Making and Unmaking of *Knock on Any Door.*" *Proof* 3 (1973): 121–37.

McIntyre, Alfred R. "The Crisis in Book Publishing." *Atlantic Monthly* 180 (Oct. 1947): 107–10.

Madison, Charles A. "Jews in American Publishing." *Chicago Jewish Forum* 26 (Summer 1968): 282–87.

Rawson, Hugh. "What Authors Should Know about Publishing Economics." 2 parts. *Authors Guild Bulletin,* Winter 1982–83, Spring 1983.

Romano, Carlin. "Whose Book Is It, Anyway?" *Philadelphia Inquirer,* 21 Sept. 1982, pp. E1, 4.

Silver, Rollo G. "The Costs of Mathew Carey's Printing Equipment." *Studies in Bibliography* 19 (1966): 85–122.

———. "Prologue to Copyright in America: 1772." *Studies in Bibliography* 11 (1958): 259–62.

"The Star System in Publishing." *Dial* 28 (16 May 1900): 389–91.

"The Writer's State." Special issue of the *Nation* 233 (3 Oct. 1981).

Index